Southern Homemade

by Lorraine Leggett Lott

Hearts 'N' Tummies Cookbook Co.
3544 Blakslee St.
Wever, IA 52658
1-800-571-2665

For my mother,
Myrrh-Lorraine Gibson Leggett,
the best cook I've ever known,

and

In Memory of
Marion Leggett Murphy

She awed us with her immense talent,
She exasperated us with her endless compulsions,
She beguiled us with her instinctive style,
She entertained us with her wry wit,
She was a beloved daughter,
caring sister,
loving aunt,
trusted friend,
and mother.
She devastated us by leaving too soon.

1946-1993

III

IV

Introduction

I still daydream about picking cotton. Sometimes if I'm gardening and I get into a briar I remember the wicked sharp thorns on the bolls of cotton. Then I shiver as I think of dragging the big sacks filled with cotton through the dusty red clay fields of Southern Mississippi. I can almost feel my sweaty palms covered with socks to protect from the miserable cotton quills. It seemed then that the plants had personalities that were filled with venom. With their dying energy they would lash out at us poor humans who'd forced them to swelter in the fields all summer. We were paid $1.00 per 100 pounds of cotton. That worked out to less than 10¢ an hour with us each picking about 100 pounds in a 12 hour day. My husband's cousin, Ted Lott, boasted of picking 300 pounds a day. How he did it we could never figure. Regardless, it was a pittance for a half year's hard labor in the fields. Had we known anything about the outside world back then, we'd have surely thought we were in hell. The cotton wasn't the only evil we had to deal with in the country. I can still see the snakes that slithered up from the swamps. I'd freeze whenever I saw a Mississippi Cobra inflate its head. To this day I have a phobia of anything that even resembles a snake. Sometimes I still hear the flies and feel the heat. But most of all I daydream about the cool iced tea and sugar cane sticks and the wonderful homemade delights that rewarded our seemingly endless work in the fields.

I was raised poor in rural Southern Mississippi. My husband's family lived down the hill from our tin roof house. His family had their own tiny wooden home and their own fields to work. Though we lived only a half mile from one another we never really knew one another back then. His family was Baptist, we were Methodists. That indirectly influenced who we socialized with in the little free time we had away from work and school. Everyone was busy surviving. My seven brothers and sisters and I love to get together from time to time at the fish camp or one of the old family diners that still serve up authentic Southern fare and relive the endless summers in the cotton fields, the sprinkling of snow falling on our beds (through cracks in the roof and walls), or better, the wonderful food that our mama would prepare despite our often desperate financial situation.

We never thought that things would change much in the South, but these days we are surprised to see fast food restaurants moving into once-rural areas. Our favorite diner is nearly empty most days, drained of customers by Dominos Pizza and the Taco Bell on once-rural Highway 49. We ponder what will happen in another generation. Will main street disappear in favor of Home Depot and Wal Mart? Will my grandchildren have any concept of the life we once lived? Will they know anything about our unique culture or will their only knowledge of the old South be one fictionalized by Hollywood. Those thoughts prompted me to begin collecting my memories and recipes of the old days and old Southern ways.

My family and I began sharing with other Southerners our fear that the old ways and the old recipes from Mississippi and other parts of the South would die with our generation. Quickly our Southern heritage started coming together in this book of traditional Southern recipes.

The art of being Southern and the Southern style of cooking may eventually become completely assimilated into American pop culture and cuisine. Therefore I begin this book with a chapter on Southern Style. Therein I relate what it means to be "Southern." I describe one of the Southern cooks best kept secrets; how to put on a stunning breakfast, dinner, or supper. In the 1940s when I was coming up we knew few rules; hospitality being the only carved-in-stone commandment. The quickest way to tell a true Southern cook is by their table, not necessarily the food they are serving. In the South one doesn't often eat off of paper. If guests are at the table, supper is on the good china with linen tablecloths. Things are bought to be used, not to be locked away in cabinets. Another dead giveaway is how a Southern host(ess) treats their guests. Guests are welcomed and encouraged to stay, and food and drink is constantly flowing from the kitchen to the gallery to the table. Many Southern families still say their prayers before meals with all hands joined around the table. Finally, the oldest member of the gathering always gets the first bite of the heaping-full dishes. A Southern cook usually has plenty of leftovers to share with their neighbors.

So many of our fine traditions have passed by the wayside as our culture has gone from one of sustenance to one that consumes and discards with abandon. Not in the South. Everything left at the table is either used, or recycled; sometimes in the garden, more often fed to the family's livestock.

Our home was made of piecemeal lumber. That is lumber left over from real houses or from ones that had collapsed or burned down. The tin roof was "recycled" as well. The boys would turn the tin sheets they found upside down, so that the original nail holes were pointing upward. Thus most of the rainwater would flow past the holes in the roof. I can remember mama bringing out the fine white linen that her aunts Betty and Luella or her sister Oneida in New Orleans had given her, when the preacher would come for noon dinner once a year. At one such special dinner the table was beautifully set. We kids had made decorations out of old newspapers that someone had dropped by the house. We were so proud of how the parlor (or front room) looked, until it came a thunderstorm. We rushed to find suitable receptacles for all of the streams of water pouring through that contemptible tin roof. The preacher never said a word and dinner went on as if there weren't a thousand tiny streams of water cascading from the ceiling. That type of graciousness, sometimes under fire, typifies Southern Style. A real-life "under fire or rain" episode which my sister would say separated those with style from those without, "you either have it or you don't. It can't be created," she'd say.

I follow with chapters that follow Southern days in the country; Backwoods Breakfasts, Dirtwater Dinners (Lunch), and Friday at the Fishcamp. This non-traditional organization corresponds to true Southerners' daily lives, not the rather odd format that most cookbooks take, grouping different parts of a meal in different sections of the book. **Backwoods Breakfasts** looks at the colorful (literal and figurative) history of grits along with some other breakfast foods a Southerner might eat. **Dirtwater Dinners** (lunches to non-Southern readers) consist largely of light salads and fruit dishes. It has always been important to not get filled up on dinner, especially during growing season, because after dinner a true Southerner often has another eight hours of work, until sundown, before supper. **Friday at the Fishcamp** includes my favorite catfish recipes. Southerners have a love affair with catfish that is quickly expanding nationally. We also like our hush puppies, sweet tea, and coffee-flavored ice cream desserts. The Fishcamp is a meeting place and a social even in addition to being a great meal. While my description could fill several cookbooks I try to limit my selections to the very best the Fishcamp has to offer.

Most non-natives equate Mississippi's cuisine with pecans. Though the perception is largely a myth, I indulge the many of the pecan recipes that have been handed down in my family. I call the chapter **Southern Nuts** because we mostly ate less valuable nuts and that title allows me to describe some of my favorite less-than-sane relations who I deem deserving of some degree of ennobling in this book.

There remain many pecan orchards in Mississippi, but, in our day the nuts were largely unavailable to most residents because of their value. Instead, we would attempt to use the very tough to crack wild hickory nuts. The stories of trying to break those nuts free from their guarded shells are almost more endearing than the recipes for the occasional pecan pie or pecan chicken that we did have as children. I remember thinking I'd cracked teeth on the shells that inevitably became imbedded in the hickory nuts that we were able to wrench free from their shells. Regardless, times became somewhat better during the 1950s and 1960s and Mississippians developed a surplus of recipes using pecans.

In Chapter 6 I indulge my favorite Dinner-on-the-Ground recipes. Sunday is a revered time in the South. We go to church, have big dinners and lay around all afternoon, enjoying our day of rest, until supper of course. Dinner-on-the-Ground is a dying Southern tradition. Too often young people are too busy or too interested in the outside world to participate in what was once our favorite social gathering. All the families in the church would bring their special entrees for a huge dinner under the huge oak tree after Sunday services. We'd eat enough to last us until Tuesday. That is if our mama wasn't watching. Eminence, our little church which sits miles from town on a quiet country road that runs from near Collins to near Laurel, Mississippi, remains unchanged in the 50 years since I was a child. Unchanged except for the absence of Dinner-on-the-Ground. Sunday suppers would be incomplete without dessert, so I follow-up with **Mississippi Mud and other Mississippi Homemade Desserts to Die For.**

A book on authentic Southern cooking would be unfinished without a look at **Button Poppin' Fried Favorites** though today it is politically, and perhaps, medically incorrect to placate oneself with the delicious fried fare that is native to the South. I can't remember a day when we were young that we didn't eat something fried. We still indulge from time to time in a slice of fresh fried pound cake, or a fried chicken dinner. When I was four or five years old my brothers told me that I could curl my straight-as-a-board hair if I'd eat the burnt portions of the fish cakes that my sisters and I would prepare for Sunday supper. Mama would buy salmon, tuna, or whitefish in the can and we'd mash it up, bones and all until it was a consistently mushy mixture. Then we'd add eggs and flour or cornmeal to create a doughy bread that we fried as fish cakes. Mama called it "Tall Fish." She nor anyone else can tell me how or why it got that name. Some of the cakes would end up burnt and I'd always snap them up first, hoping my hair would curl into a perfect Shirley Temple "do." I guess I was nine or ten before I realized that the burnt fish wasn't helping my hairstyle any. When I look at today's children and how fast they grow up I remember fondly the naivety of our youth. It was a slower, much simpler time. We didn't know any better than to eat everything fried in lard and besides, it was all we had back then. I know many of my aunts and uncles lived well into their nineties having spent their life eating consistently greasy Southern fare that included lots and lots of pork. In the interest of supposedly "good" health I include just a sampling of our fried favorites.

In Chapter 9 I detail some of the South's favorite seafood recipes that don't include catfish. **Bayou to Bay Seafood Favorites** looks at the coastal favorites from throughout the Southeastern United States. Finally **Southern Holidays** are described in Chapter 10. Of course, I saved the best for last. I was born on Christmas day, my mama says it was because she had too much turkey at dinner. I also got married on Christmas Day. Needless to say, Christmas has always been special in the South, but for me it has taken on treble significance. I remember our search for the perfect holly tree to decorate our parlor. We couldn't afford decorations, so the holly berries provided free holiday color. We would grow a little popping corn every year just to have enough to string for the tree. Old newspaper dipped in a mixture of colored flour and water was cut and pieced together to make Christmas garland. Anything else we could find that was pretty and had some color would be hung from the branches of the holly tree. We felt like kings and queens when we were given $2.50 each at Christmas to buy something special for ourselves. Mama would save pennies all year to present us with that money. She'd also have something special for each of us that she'd ordered out of the Sears catalog. Then we'd go to Main Street and buy some special item we'd had our eye on for months. Imagine what our grandchildren's reaction would be if all they received for Christmas was $20.00. What would they do if they had to make their own butter, milk, bread, etc. Ironically, history has a way of repeating itself. I hope that this book serves as a guide to our ancestors should they ever become what I not-so-fondly label survival (or subsistence) farmers again. And if not, I know the book will offer many unique recipes for those who just love to cook. Enjoy.

Chapter 1
Southern Style

A while back a friend asked me what it meant to be Southern. My friend, an author and a transplant from the North, was working on a local newspaper's Sunday Magazine article that focused on Northerners who had moved to the South, permanently. In the article she wanted to talk about her new roots in the South. However, her editor thought that the article should focus instead on her Northern heritage and difficulties she had experienced adjusting to Southern ways. He specifically mentioned our checkered history. I could feel my anger rising as she explained that the South to him was all about slavery, corruption, and intolerance. She argued that she couldn't think of any problems relating to her new Southern neighbors. She said Southerners were so "friendly, and approachable," very unlike Northerners. She asked me what being Southern meant to me. I couldn't immediately answer but I did begin trying to paint a mental picture of what it meant to be Southern. It seemed that geographic lines drawn hundreds of years ago first popped into my head. Of course the South is more than a geographical area, more than mockingbirds and magnolias, more than mint juleps and the Kentucky Derby, even more than catfish and hush puppies. But where does a Southern start trying to describe what is really best defined as a state of mind? I started with the geography we'd learned as kids.

Truly the South, or Dixie as we Southerners prefer to call it, is a geographical region. Technically, everything in the Eastern United States South of the Mason-Dixon Line belongs to the South. The line was originally drawn by two British astronomers, Charles Mason and Jeremiah Dixon. They had no idea that their work (1763-67) would eventually take on its infamous distinction. Their job was to delineate the boundary between Pennsylvania and Maryland to settle a dispute between the Calvert family, proprietors of Maryland, and the Penn family, proprietors of Pennsylvania.

The line earned its North-South distinction much later, in 1820 when Congress debated the Missouri Compromise. That legislation forbade slavery in the Louisiana Territory north of the parallel 36°30', except in Missouri. In that sense, the Mason-Dixon Line meant not only the old disputed boundary line but also the line of the Ohio river from the Pennsylvania boundary to its mouth, where it flows into the Mississippi River, then the east, north, and west boundaries of Missouri, and from that point westward. So geographically, the South includes Maryland, West Virginia, Missouri, Kentucky, Virginia, the Carolinas, Tennessee, Arkansas, Texas, Louisiana, Mississippi, Alabama, Georgia, and Florida. That's a lot of territory with a lot of subcultural heritage in smaller geographic subregions (the Appalachians, the Piney Woods, the Coastal Plains, etcetera) within the South. A few states have new ties to other regions. Peninsular Florida, for example, has become cosmopolitan and influenced more by Latin Americans than by Southerners. The Atlanta area of Georgia, similarly, is part of the New South, brimming with all things Northern, Western, and moreover, Modern. I wouldn't consider Maryland part of the South, rather mid-Atlantic and certainly Texas' ties are stronger to Western and Mexican cultures.

Others would define the South historically, by the eleven states that seceded from the United States to form the Confederate States of America, which included Texas. By this point in my growing Southern diatribe my friend was really shaking her head. Defining Southernness was going to be harder than either of us first thought. My friend wisely changed the subject, asking the origin of the term Dixie. We've all used it for years but it took some brain-rattling and then remembering some of the wonderful Cajun cuisine that my aunts and uncles in New Orleans prepared for us as children to jog my memory.

Dixie, is the popular name for the American South. One story goes that it is derived from the French "dix" (ten) which was inscribed on the back of $10 bills issued by the Citizens' Bank of Louisiana before the Civil War. That's the anecdote my Aunt Ethel told me more than once. Dixie brings to mind stories of slavery, intolerance, and corruption; all arguably part of our Southern heritage as well. My family came up poor in rural Mississippi. We were so poor that we knew little of racial intolerance. We knew even less about corruption, something that went largely unnoticed by our clan who's collective goal was to grow enough food to eat in a group effort to survive. With today's instantaneous satellite transmission of current events we are much more aware of prejudice, racial inequalities, and abuses of power than in the days that formed our Southern memories.

Being Southern, to me, has much more to do with a kind, genteel, self-sufficiency and style that largely escapes today's younger generations. It is a frame of reference that features family, religion, and community. It is a courteous, respectful state of mind. I've attempted to instill those values in all of my children. We've also taught them how to be self-sufficient. They all know how to garden, how to farm, and how to cook should the day ever come that we're all forced back into that lifestyle. While none of my children chose to continue the family farm, we keep the land and know that if we had to, we could largely take care of ourselves without the help of anyone aside from our rural neighbors. Therein lie our closest ties to the South and our deepest memories. Picking cotton, making homemade cornbread, fresh vegetables, working the fields, and community and religious gatherings. Those food-related memories concrete my memories of a Southern childhood. But its not just me and my family's struggles that center around Southern edible events. As I thought harder I could remember how mealtimes were the most important times of the Southern day. It was then that the family came together and communicated. Other edible affairs occur with an age old regularity in the South. The whole community gets together for Sunday dinners and suppers or Dinner-on-the-Ground as we call it. Fish Camps offer a mid-week break and fraternization session for Southern communities. Family get-togethers are always dominated by even more. . . food. So my friend asked if I could sum up Southernness in a paragraph.

"Impossible. But I'll try," I responded now growing irritated with her for cutting short my Southern stories. Irritated that she, a Northerner, should think that our way of life could be partitioned into a paragraph.

I tried unsuccessfully. I began, "we are geographically distinct, we love homemade food served with some regularity. We also share a close-knit community and family life. Being Southern in the old days meant knowing all of your relatives and not hiding any of the crazy ones out in the smoke house when company came to visit. It also meant knowing all of your neighbors, and their relations as well. Being Southern meant if any of the above-mentioned family or neighbors were sick or if someone died the community would spontaneously converge on the person's home with cakes, casseroles, snacks, and beverages. Being Southern meant Sunday Supper would be a special family time, that Friday's would be spent at the Fish Camp, and that despite our often dire financial situation, dinner, when company arrived from New Orleans or Birmingham, would be served on fine linen table cloths. You could see the sun peak through the roof of our tin roof house, but you'd not find a finer table setting in the County than what my mama would prepare on special occasions."

"Well," I mused, I'd summed it up in a long paragraph but I'd forgotten one of our most endearing traits: Our unique language. The dialect in the part of the South where I was raised differs drastically from Louisiana, which today is less than a two hour drive. Similarly, the Appalachians are chock-full of distinct tongues. My children have little, if any, of our Southern drawl, which I think is very sad. I like nothing better than sitting down with my sister Bette who slings colloquialisms faster than flies lighting on . . . well, you get the picture. Our language is part of what identifies us as Southerners, and more directly as being from the Ozarks, the Bayou Country, or the Delta.

Being Southern is therefore many things. Most important to me is keeping the family traditions alive and keeping the communities together. That may sound easy enough but in reality it is an increasingly difficult task as the Modern world encroaches ever closer to our hidden Southern hamlets. The way we commune has changed little. Homemade consumables bring us all together. It seems that community, family, and friends are more easily remembered when I was looking over one of my dog-eared, age old cookbooks. That spirit of togetherness, at least at dinner-time, is one of the enduring traditions that define the South for me. So my friend by now is reclined on the couch, rubbing her temples. She asked, "can't you just give it to me in a sound-bite, a one-liner. . . a quip?" Nope. Can't be done! Southern style is somewhat easier to sum up.

How does one achieve Southern style? Three words: Practice relaxed elegance. In this chapter I serve up some tips on putting on the Southern treatment when dealing with mealtime (no matter which mealtime, mind you) guests. I also remember my mother-in-law Gladys and my husband's grandmother Ada, two relations who personified Southern Style.

There is more to Southern style than just cooking a good homemade meal. Southern cooks don't purchase paper plates. Everything is served on the good china, with the good crystal, and the fine flatware. We take a little more time and expend a lot more effort to ensure that everyone leaves the table full, and with pleasant memories of their visit. Southern meals are a happening, not just a eat-and-run affair. That is if they're done right!

A little practice with the dying art of napkin folding can really dress up any table. At the beginning of the breakfast, dinner, and supper chapters I provide the proper table setting for those meals. Whole volumes have been written on napkin folding which is nothing more than a presentation detail. I say detail because it doesn't matter if you bother or not, it just adds a special touch if you have the time and energy to do so.

Napkin Folding

Just about any kind of napkin can be folded. It helps if the napkin is fabric (though paper will do just fine), is square, well pressed, and lightly starched. For informal affairs colorful print napkins are delightful. For formal suppers an elegant look is achieved with lace-trimmed, embroidered, or tailored linen napkins.

The Basic Fold

The basic fold is just as it sounds. In the South, especially when company's coming, we try to dress up the presentation at least this much. . . . Note: This is EXTREMELY EASY!! Go ahead and give it a try.

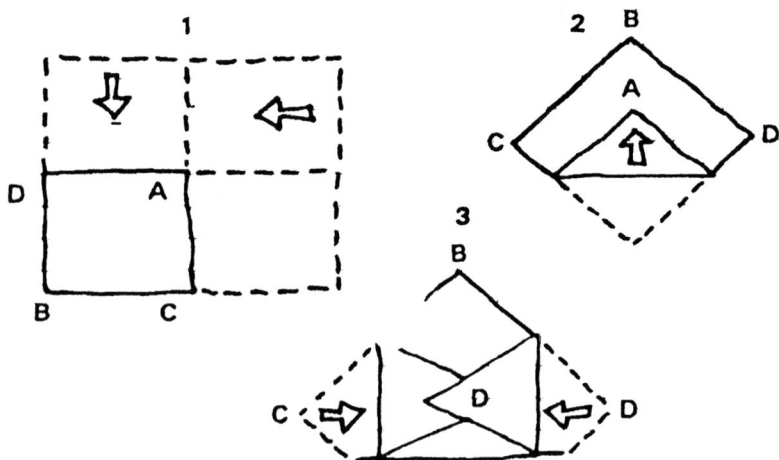

If this one gives you trouble you might just as well stick with folded triangles as is the custom in many homes. I'm not great with my hands but at a recent impromptu cookout I managed to create a number of different folds using a guide like the one above and quickly folding while directing other "cooks."

These instructions walk you through a step-by-step Basic Fold.

1. Fold napkin in half and then into quarter size (ACBD).
2. Turn up folded corner (A) three quarters of the way to point (B).
3. Fold points (C) and (D) toward the center and overlap.
4. Turn the napkin over. Make sure sides are even and point (B) is in the center.
5. Use as is or turn down corners at point (B) to reveal lace or embroidered corner

Once you've mastered the basic fold you'll be dying to try something a little more challenging. The Crosstie and Buffet Knots are almost as easy but look very elegant. These are particularly useful and attractive on buffet-style tables.

The Crosstie

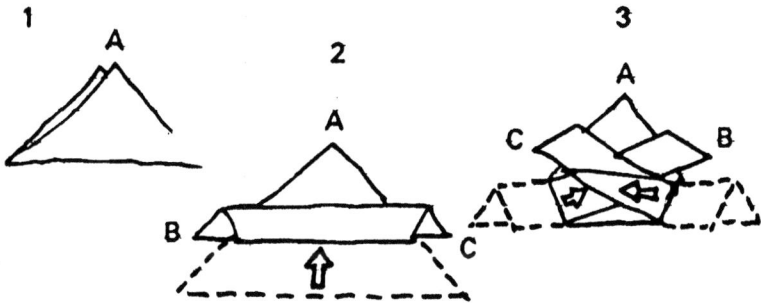

1. Fold napkin into a large triangle with center point (A) at the top.
2. Turn fold at base of triangle up ¼ from the bottom. Fold up an additional ¼.
3. Cross point (B) and point (C).

The Buffet Knot

The **Buffet Knot** looks elegant but is a cinch. This doesn't work too well with paper napkins unless you're using one of the fancier varieties found adjacent to the very good paper plates in the supermarket. This is basically one fold, a roll, and a knot. Lay the finished napkin across the dinner plate.

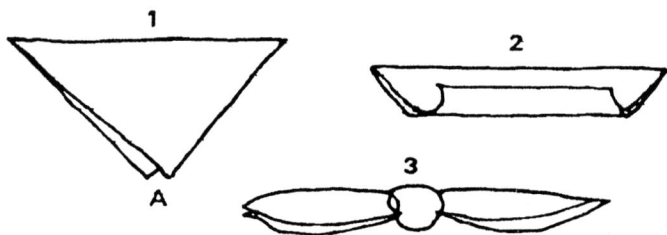

1. Fold napkin into a triangle with center point (A) at the bottom.
2. Roll napkin up beginning at point (A).
3. Tie a knot at the center of rolled napkin. What could be easier?!

The Buffet Silver Server

The **Buffet Silver Server** is one of my favorite ways to tidy up the table. A simple fold and tuck the silverware right into the napkins. I used this fold at a recent family dinner and had all the gang asking where the silverware was. I'd used large paper napkins and no knives. The bulk of the silverware wasn't visible. I decided next time, for informal affairs, I'd try colored party napkins folded into the **Silver Server**. Whether you're have two or two hundred to dinner folded napkins will always draw more raves than your immaculate house or tasteful decorations!

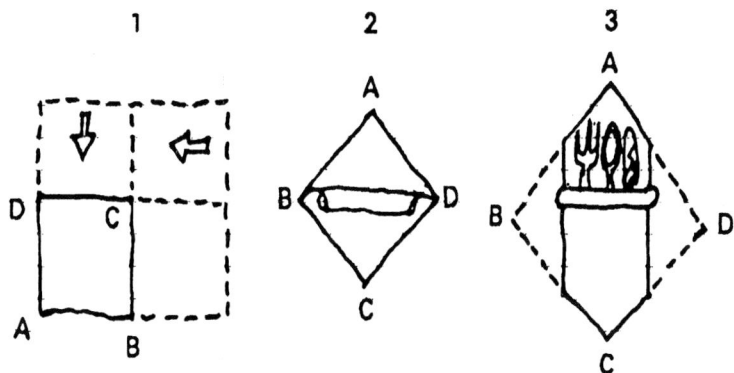

1. Fold napkin in half and then into quarter size (ABCD).
2. Roll two of the four top flaps (A) halfway down the napkin.
3. Fold point (B) and point (D) under. Make sure points (A) and (C) are in the center of the folded napkin. Silver may be placed in the pocket.

By now you're getting the idea that this is really pretty easy! The final napkin I'll share with you may take a little more practice. The Standing Crown is great for more formal affairs like Sunday Supper or Holiday Meals. You may want to make note of some napkin folding hints before attempting this last fold: Work on a clean, hard surface and press firmly so that the finished folds are crisp. Lightly press the folds if they won't stay put. While it is most desirable to use linen napkins, any woven cloth or even paper napkins can be utilized. The only secret is that the napkin should be a true square and not limp!

Use colored napkins and matching candles to liven up any meal. Also try throwing colorful leaves from your flowers on the table. Petals scattered over the table offer a nice touch as well. For the finishing touch take a large bowl filled with water and float a few candles in the center of the table. For a few minutes, at least, your guests will be awe-struck. . . . at least until the first course.

The Standing Crown

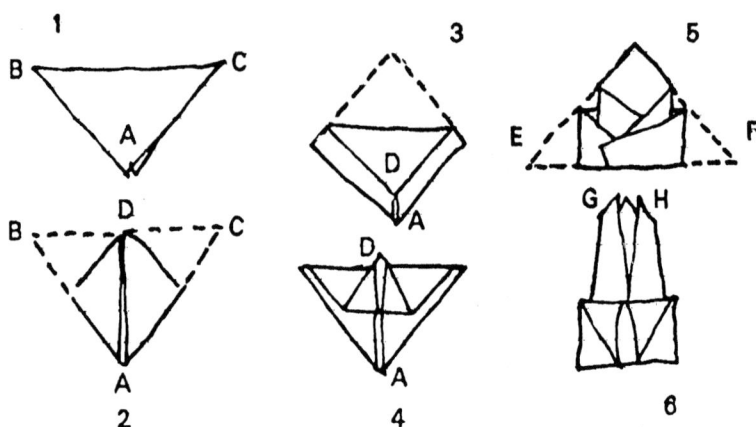

1. Fold napkin into a triangle with the center point (A) at bottom.
2. Fold point (B) and point (C) to meet center point (A).
3. Fold top corner (D) down to within one inch of center point (A).
4. Turn the folded point (D) back to upper edge.
5. Turn napkin over. Fold and overlap left corner (E) and right corner (F). Place one corner inside the other one.
6. Stand up as is or create a flower effect by folding down upper corners (G) and (H).

At Christmas try the **Standing Crown** using red and green linen napkins. For Thanksgiving use gold, brown, or beige. Easter dinners look great with colorful pastels or for the religious celebration choose lavender, yellow, and white. For summer choose bright linen prints and dazzle your guests when they see your beautifully set table.

There are a number of inexpensive books on napkin folding available from any of the national-chain bookstores. There are hundreds of folding styles to choose from.

When I think of a person that most embodies(ed) what I think of as Southern style my mother-in-law Gladys always comes to mind. She left the home place in the 1940s when her husband joined the armed forces. They took the family to Pensacola, Florida's Navy Point. It was a collection of modest homes just off of the huge Naval Air Station. Whenever we went to visit her at her tiny home, she would bring out the fine china and linen table cloths and napkins. In her pint-sized kitchen there was room for only one set of hands. Every burner on the stove would be red hot while she worked nonstop, the thick coffee would be brewing, and the stories would drift through the warm moist air along with the aroma of a collection of unique homemade delights. I would sit in the old wrought iron rocking couch on her front porch, listening to the wind whistling in the long-needle pines, and my mind would drift back to Nubbin Ridge and my husband's grandmother's house near Seminary, Mississippi in what was referred to locally as the Eminence Community.

I remember Grandma Ada taking a large cast iron pot, slamming it down on the wood burning stove full of water from the well, and pouring in a quarter pound of coffee. She'd let it cook for hours, stirring occasionally, then ladle direct from the iron pot to the ceramic coffee mugs. Half of the cup would be "mud" as we called it, but the top half was great, rich, coffee. No one ever had to ask Ada for coffee. It was always warm on the stove. We joked that she kept the caffeine flowing so that we'd have energy to finish the long lists of chores that she'd give us all to do, even after we were grown with families of our own to tend. We politely obliged, drinking more of the real Mississippi Mud for inspiration.

To put a guest at ease one must be at ease themselves. A true Southerner's home is clean, but perhaps not neat. A "lived in" feel is what most impresses the first time visitor to Southern Homes. It's often difficult to achieve that look and feel when it is 90° F. in the shade and 90% humidity *and* dusty red clay is blowing in the haze. Abundant drinks are a must.

Some of my fondest memories of childhood are of my father sitting on the gallery (front porch) of our home, cutting people's hair for 25¢, telling and listening to all of the week's gossip. Mama would make tea in a big old enameled pot. She would dump tea into the pot of boiling water, then after a while she'd drain it and add more water and sugar until it tasted just right. We didn't have anything like tea bags back then. The following is as close to the old recipe as possible, using modern conveniences.

Summer Iced Tea

8 tea bags ~ 5 slices of lemon
1 gallon of boiling water ~ 2 cups of sugar

Steep the tea in and lemon in boiling water for about 10 minutes. Remove tea bags from water. Add sugar and stir. Makes 1 gallon. Served iced, and start the next pot.

Of course, Daddy drank plenty, but many Southerners are and have always been teetotalers. The Eminence Community (near the present day Jones-Covington county line in South-Central Mississippi) was, and still is, dry. That is to say that liquor is never sold there. We substituted fresh berries where others would insert alcohol. For example, one Southern favorite, Strawberry Soup, is often served with a dry red wine. Instead, we make it like this:

Strawberry Soup

1 cup fresh strawberries ~ ¼ cup honey
¼ cup sour cream ~ 1½ cups cold water

Mix all ingredients in blender or beat vigorously with fork until nearly liquefied. Small seeds will be visible but need only be strained for those who seeds are a problem. Chill and serve. This recipe will serve four. In our family we multiply the ingredients by four in order to get a heaping supply.

There were other teas, often spiced, that perked us up for hot afternoons of working the fields. They symbolize Southern style and were often saved for special occasions, the hottest days, or for unexpected guests because of the cost and scarcity of spices.

Spiced Citrus Tea

3 quarts water ~ 1 stick cinnamon
2 teaspoons whole cloves ~ 5 tea bags
16 oz. pineapple juice ~ 6 oz. orange juice
1¾ cups sugar ~ Juice of 2 lemons (⅓ cup)

Boil water, cinnamon and cloves for about 10 minutes. Add tea bags and let steep while mixing the pineapple juice, orange juice, lemon juice and sugar. Strain tea bags and mix all together. Makes 1 gallon.

Tangy Spiced Tea

1 cup instant tea with lemon and sugar added
2 cups sugar ~ 1 18-ounce jar Tang
1 package sweetened lemonade mix (3 oz.)
1 teaspoon ground cloves ~ 1 teaspoon cinnamon

Mix all ingredients together and store in an air tight container. Use 2 heaping teaspoons for regular cup and 3 heaping teaspoons for mug. Add boiling water and stir. For 1 chilled gallon take two cups of mixture, add boiling water and stir. Chill and serve cold.

For an authentic special occasion tea you might like to try tea syrup, the way we made it before refrigerators and electric stoves. I can't tell you how many times I've talked to one of the kids about the days before electricity made it to our neck of the woods. They look at me with expressions of dumbfounded disbelief. "How did you survive" is the common inquiry? "We survived just fine," is my archetypical response.

Tea Syrup

1 quart water ~ ½ cup loose tea ~ 2 cups sugar

Mix water and tea and bring to a boil. Steep six minutes and strain. Add sugar. Can syrup.

To make iced tea from syrup add 1 quart of water to each cup of syrup. May add more sugar for a very sweet tea.

Flavored teas were a novelty in my day. Now they are all the rage. Take the following recipe and substitute your favorite berry (in place of cranberries) for a delicious flavored iced tea.

Cranberry Tea

1 pound cranberries ~ 1 quart water ~ 2 cups sugar
3 sticks cinnamon ~ 2 cups orange juice
3 Tablespoons lemon juice ~ ½ teaspoon salt

Cook berries in 2 cups of water, until berries pop. Strain through a colander. Bring 2 cups sugar, 2 cups water, and cinnamon sticks to a rolling boil. Add strained berries to the mixture along with juices and salt. Serve hot or cold. Makes ½ gallon.

Finally, every Southerner can remember some variation of Gingerberry Punch from their childhood. Basically one used whatever berries were available. In the South we're blessed with an abundant supply of blueberries, huckleberries, blackberries, strawberries, and other wild berries. I can remember the fun my sisters and I had climbing through the tall pines in search of blackberries. We'd eat two for every one that got into our baskets. Then when Mama asked where all the berries were we'd hold our mouths tightly shut and project our best baffled expressions, terrified that she'd see our purple-black mouths. Little did we know that she could see the blackberry stains all over our faces. Dainty we were not! This is my family's "mix."

Gingerberry Punch

1 16-ounce can or package frozen strawberries
1 6-ounce can frozen orange juice concentrate
1 6-ounce can frozen lemonade concentrate
1 12-ounce bottle ginger ale
1 cup whole fresh strawberries
3 orange slices ~ 3 cups water

Thaw strawberries while combining orange juice, lemonade and water. Chill thoroughly. Freeze 2 cups of the punch. When ready to serve add thawed strawberries and ginger ale. Then add frozen punch and garnish with fresh strawberries and orange slices.

There are other ways to put on the Southern Style that are simple and unique. One of my favorites, after the drinks and table settings, is to create daffodils, daisies, rosebuds, and zinnas out of turnips, radishes, and cheese. Culinarily speaking these are fancy garnishes. A more festive table is created when the Southern cook adds that little special touch.

Garnishes can range from a little parsley or kale to a spray of white turnip zinnias. All can be purchased, prepared, and stored for up to a week in advance. Entire volumes have been written on this subject as well. Here I'll share just two of my favorites.

First you'll need a corrugated-edge slicer. These can be found at any store that sells cheese graters and the like. You'll also need a vegetable cutter. Its an odd looking gadget that comes in many forms and price ranges. Ask the clerk for the cheap old-fashioned one. Then you'll feel extra proud of your end product.

Garnishes

Zinnias

You'll need the following to prepare delightful zinnias for your next supper:

A thin-slice vegetable cutter
A corrugated-edge vegetable slicer
Scissors
Large white turnips (NO POTATOES)
Small carrots-cleaned
Toothpicks
Food coloring

Using the vegetable cutter, cut 3 thin slices of white turnip, varying about ⅓-inch in size. With scissors, cut approximately 12 "petals" in each slice. Round off the corners of the petals. Place cut turnip slices in a bowl of ice water containing food coloring of your choice. Using the corrugated-edge slicer, cut a small carrot cross-wise into slices about ½-inch thick. Stick a toothpick into one end of the carrot, and then slide on the smallest turnip slice, the next largest, and the largest, pushing the all close together.

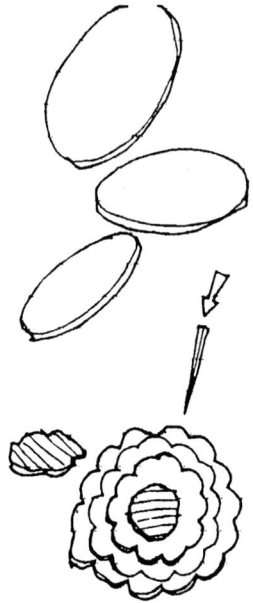

Place the finished zinnias in a large plastic container with a tight-fitting top for storage if prepared ahead. Three days ahead is best but they will keep up to a week if you cover the florets with damp paper towels and keep the container tightly closed and refrigerated. Potatoes won't work because they quickly turn brown when exposed to atmosphere. Use the zinnias as part of a centerpiece or on each plate as an added personal touch to the dinner presentation. Next try Radish Rosebuds.

Radish Rosebuds

You'll need the following to prepare radish rosebuds:

a sharp knife
radishes

Wash radishes and remove a small, thin slice from each end of the radish. Form petals by cutting v-shaped slits, all the way around the radish, starting at the top and cutting down about ⅔ the length of the radish. Using the tip of the knife, carefully cut around the inside edge of the radish, to free the petals. Gently remove the v-shaped portions of the radish peel, between the petals. Store in ice water in refrigerator for up to a week.

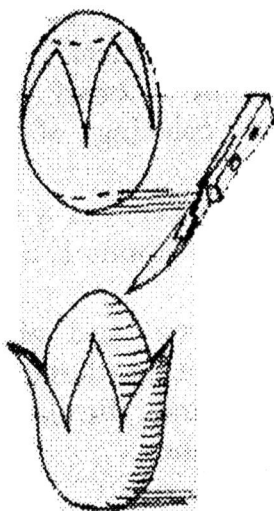

Cheese Rosebuds

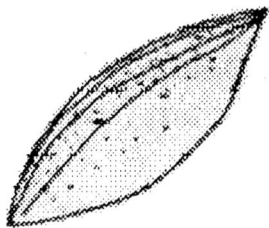

You'll need the following to prepare cheese rosebuds:

mild cheddar cheese, grated
stuffed olives
scissors
toothpicks, frilly
red food coloring

Allow mild cheddar cheese to soften at room temperature, then grate. Using your fingers, shape a small amount of the cheese into a double cone. Next, remove pimiento from stuffed olives. With scissors, cut the olive to form the base of a rosebud. Insert cheese cone into olive cup, leaving half out to form the bud. Shape the bud with your fingers. Using a toothpick or a fine brush, gently streak on a small amount of red food coloring.

To serve, use frilly toothpicks, sticking one cheese rosebud one toothpick with the frills embedding into the olive base. Use to garnish anything solid on your menu.

You can also take greenery from your yard arranged in a vase and attach rosebuds to greenery as a centerpiece.

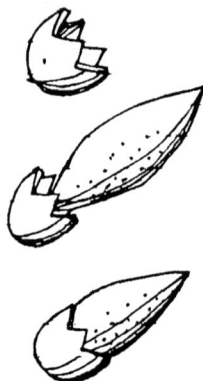

You've surely been to a party where the host(ess) served plates with daffodils, daisies, and other flowers made out of turnips. All follow the basic instructions above only with a bit more difficulty and time involved. Find a party book for dozens more ways to dress up your table with garnishes.

One of my favorites for ease of preparation and versatility of design is the watermelon boat. For that matter any kind of melon could become a boat. In a hurry you can carve a melon to look like a picnic basket, dump in some cherries, blueberries, grapes, whatever. . . and have a delightful centerpiece and nutritious dessert. If you have a little more time to prepare ahead, watermelon boats look fantastic with melon balls filling the "basket" or boat.

Now that we've tackled Southern Style, I move on to the Southern meals; breakfast, dinner, and supper. What is the main ingredient in a Southern Breakfast? Read on!

Chapter 2
Backwoods Breakfasts

Getting the Southern day started includes setting a proper table. This is a typical Southern breakfast table.

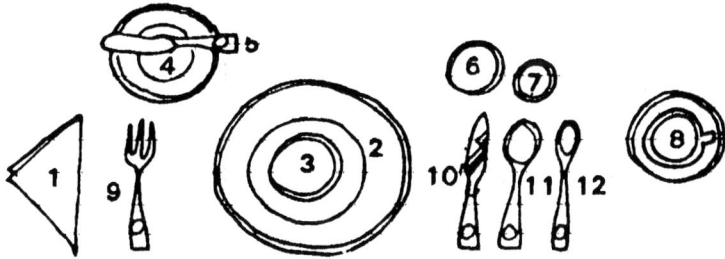

1. Napkin	7. Juice glass
2. Plate	8. Cup and saucer
3. Grits dish (also used for cereal)	9. Fork
4. Bread-and-butter plate	10. Knife
5. Butter knife	11. Cereal spoon
6. Water glass	12. Coffee or tea spoon

Once the table is set you'll want to always remember that the cornerstone of a Southern breakfast is undisputably grits. Grits are surprisingly easy to prepare, filling, and uniquely American if not an original Southern invention. Amazingly, there are experienced cooks unfamiliar with preparing grits. For them, there can be challenging moments trying to get the grits to the correct consistency. Too hard or lumpy seem to be a common complaints, while outsiders often complain that they "didn't know grits were for real." Grits are for real and can be found on supermarket shelves throughout the nation. I've found them in New York and New Mexico, I'm sure if you look hard on the flour aisle of your local supermarket, you can find them too.

Grits

Grits are basically ground or cracked hominy. Hominy is an American Indian food made from dried corn. Grits come in two varieties — cornmeal and hominy. Both are made from mature white or yellow corn from which the bran and germ have been removed. Technically cornmeal is ground corn and hominy consists of kernels of hulled corn (whole or broken). Supermarket grits are generally processed hominy. They've often been treated in an alkaline solution so that the hulls and germ float to the surface. Therefore they are "bleached." Once bleached the corn is dried, vitamin enriched and ground. Both are Native American dishes passed down on both sides of my family. However, we can't claim them all as our own. Most Southern families have their own variation of the basic recipe that has been passed down for over two centuries.

There are some basic differences in grits found in Northern and Southern states. White cornmeal and grits are traditional in the South; yellow cornmeal and grits are more likely to be found in the North. Besides color, there are also differences in the flavor of these two varieties of cornmeal. It constantly amazes me that we often take for granted the vast changes that a few decades can bring. We can remember our mothers preparing hominy in a metal tub atop the wood-burning stove. Their recipes were simple: Fill tub with hulled corn, add water to cover, add 1 cup of Lye, boil overnight. That's not a misprint. Presumably the Lye would cook off. Once you had hominy it was only a quick (all day) trip to the grist mill for grinding into cornmeal for grits. Their recipe was very close to what the early Southern settlers learned from the Native Americans. The Native Americans soaked their corn in a solution of lye made from wood ashes. Ashen grits preserved the grain through winter and spring.

Grits are one of the many foods handed down to us by generous Native Americans. The basic recipe is truly elementary!

Elementary Grits

1 quart water ~ ½ stick butter ~ Pinch salt ~ 1 cup grits

Bring the water and butter to a boil in a non-stick pot. Gradually add the grits, return to a boil, salt, then reduce to a simmer. Stir the grits occasionally to avoid sticking and skin formation. Cook for about 20 minutes until creamy (to taste). Add additional water if necessary to obtain preferred consistency.

Grits can also be cooked overnight in a crock pot (add more water) or slowly on the stove top for hours though most varieties today take 5 minutes or less to prepare. Remember, if you happen to leave the grits standing and they do stick. Soak the pot, grits and all, in water for about an hour before you try to clean-up. Grits form a concrete like concoction if left to dry. They'll crust on anything and everything from your utensils to Uncle Roy's beard.

Once you've mastered **Elementary Grits** try these fancier varieties. A favorite addition to basic grits that I've not included here is any kind of eggs (scrambled, poached, hard boiled, or sunny side up) and bacon and served alongside grits. Cook the bacon first and then cook eggs in the bacon grease to give them a nice flavor.

Cheese Grits

1½ quart greased baking dish ~ 1 cup uncooked grits
1½ Tablespoons garlic (minced) ~ 2 Tablespoons butter
1½ cups cheddar cheese, shredded ~ 3 cups water

Preheat oven to 375°F. Cook grits until creamy. In a small skillet sauté garlic in 1 Tablespoon of butter over a low heat for several minutes. Stir the garlic mixture into the grits along with the cheese until melted. Pour the mixture into baking dish and bake for 35-40 minutes or until grits are golden brown around the edges.

Simple Grits Casserole

1 cup uncooked grits ~ ¼ pound butter
¾ pound cheese (whatever variety you prefer)
½ cup milk ~ 2 eggs ~ 1 greased casserole dish

Cook grits according to package directions. After grits are cooked, stir in butter and cheese. Cool grits while beating milk into eggs. Stir milk/egg mixture into grits and pour into a buttered casserole dish. Bake at 350°F. for 45 minutes, or until browned.

Once you've mastered **Elementary Grits** and the **Simple Grits Casserole** you'll be ready to try your hand at something a little more challenging. The following four grits recipes represent just that challenge. Don't be put off by their names; **Grits Casino** and **Grits Soufflé** are almost as easy to prepare as **Elementary Grits**, but you're the only one who has to know that.

Tomorrow's Grits and Sausage Casserole

9 x 13 greased pan ~ 1½ pounds medium pork sausage
¾ cup grits ~ 6 eggs ~ 1 heaping cup milk
Pinch garlic salt ~ Pinch pepper ~ ¼ stick butter
1 slice bread ~ 1½ cups shredded sharp cheddar cheese

Cook sausage until browned, stirring to crumble. Drain and set aside. Cook grits according to package directions and set aside. In a large bowl, beat eggs well, then add milk, garlic salt and pepper and beat again. Stir in butter and crumbled bread. Stir in shredded cheese, sausage, and grits. Refrigerate overnight. When ready to prepare casserole preheat oven to 350°F. Spread mixture into greased pan. Bake uncovered for about 1 hour or until set and golden brown. Cool casserole for 10 minutes before serving.

Grits Soufflé

1 cup grits, cook after measuring
1 6-ounce Package garlic or bacon flavored cheese
3 eggs which have been broken into a 1 cup measure
1 stick butter ~ ½ cup milk
1 cup grated Cheddar cheese ~ Pinch paprika

Melt butter and ½ cup cheese and mix well with cooked grits. Make it easy on yourself, dump the butter and cheese directly into cooking grits. Whip eggs, add milk to make a complete cup, mix eggs and milk well, then combine with grits mixture. Pour into greased casserole and top with ½ cup grated cheddar cheese. Sprinkle with paprika. Bake at 350°F. for 20-30 minutes.

Garlic Grits

½ cup grits ~ 2 cups water ~ ½ Tablespoon salt
½ stick butter ~ ¼ pound garlic cheese ~ ¼ pound sharp cheese
1 Tablespoon Worcestershire sauce ~ Pinch paprika

Cook grits in water and salt. Add butter, garlic cheese, sharp cheese and Worcestershire sauce. Stir until melted. Put in greased casserole and sprinkle with paprika. Bake in 350°F. oven for 15 to 20 minutes.

Supermarket Grits

"Instant" grits are *awful*. Non-instant supermarket grits are processed hominy. They've often been treated in an alkaline solution so that the hulls and germ float to the surface. Therefore they are "bleached." Once bleached the corn is dried and ground much like the Native American recipes. One difference; processed grits are enriched making them more nutritious.

Sausage and Grits Casino

¾ cup water ~ 3 Tablespoons grits ~ ½ cup grated cheddar
1 pound medium ground sausage ~ 1½ Tablespoons oil
½ cup finely chopped bell pepper ~ 4 eggs
6 scallions sliced thin ~ Pepper to taste

Boil water, add grits and cook until grits are thick and firm. Spoon grits onto wax paper. Form into a ½ inch thick rectangle. Chill for 15 minutes. Cut grits into ½ inch "dice." In a skillet, cook sausage and bell pepper in 1 Tablespoon of oil. Crumble sausage while cooking. When browned, drain and leave in skillet. In a bowl whisk together eggs, scallions, cheese, and pepper. Next, replace sausage skillet on burner, add 1 Tablespoon oil and reheat, spreading the sausage evenly on the bottom of skillet. Gently place grits dice atop cooking sausage. Carefully pour in egg/cheese mixture and cook for 8-10 minutes on low heat until center is set. Cool for 5 minutes, cut into wedges and serve warm.

Southerners do eat biscuits with their grits. It seems strange to outsiders to see us stacking our starches but biscuits are an important part of many Southern meals. For breakfast I provide several homemade biscuit recipes. These are just your basic farm-made biscuit recipes. Of course they get old after awhile and you'll want to dress them up so I follow-up with two dressed-up Southern biscuits. You might want to experiment with meal-sized biscuits as well!

Meal-Sized Biscuits

In the old days Southern cooks would often prepare huge biscuits that dwarf the trendy supermarket "jumbo" canned biscuits. They'd be served as a meal, topped with homemade molasses or preserves. You can create meal-sized biscuits by rolling out 2-inch thick (or thicker) dough instead of the standard ½-inch sized biscuits described below. Play with oven temperature and baking times.

Plain Biscuits

2 cups self-rising flour ~ ½ cup solid shortening ~ ¾ cup milk

Place flour and shortening in large mixing bowl. Cut in with fork until consistency of coarse cornmeal. Add milk. Stir with fork until mixture leaves sides of bowl and forms a soft, moist dough. Place dough on floured surface; sprinkle dough lightly with flour. Kneed gently until no longer sticky. Roll out until ½-inch thick. Cut with 2-inch floured cutter. Place on ungreased baking sheet and bake at 450°F. for about 10 minutes until golden brown.

If you find **Plain Biscuits** are just too drab for your diet, you might prefer **Quick Mix Biscuits**. The two recipes are almost identical except **Quick Mix Biscuits** are lighter and dryer. Top either of these rather basic biscuits with fresh homemade molasses to please the sweet tooths in your family.

Quick Mix Biscuits

2 cups self-rising flour ~ ¼ cup soft shortening ~ ½ cup milk

Put flour into a 2-quart bowl. Make a well in center of flour mixture. Add shortening and milk. Stir with a fork until mixture leaves sides of bowl and has taken up all the flour. Turn onto lightly floured board. Work gently with floured hands. Shape dough into a ball. Pat down until ½ inch thick. Fold in half. Pat down again to form as 8 x 6-inch rectangle about ½-inch thick. Cut with a 2-inch floured cutter. Cut as close together as possible. Push scraps together and shape into biscuit rounds. Put on ungreased baking pan. Bake on oven rack slightly above center at 450°F. about 10 minutes, or until light brown. Makes 16 biscuits.

The following recipe gets its name because the finished product comes out looking something like the muddy color of the Mississippi River.

Mississippi River Biscuits

4 cups plain flour ~ 4 teaspoons baking powder
4 teaspoons sugar ~ 1 teaspoon salt
2 cakes of yeast or 2 packages of dry yeast
2 cups milk ~ 4 teaspoons shortening
4 Tablespoons cinnamon ~ 2 Tablespoons nutmeg

Dissolve yeast in warm milk. Add other ingredients. Mix, then knead. Brush both sides of dough with melted butter. Fold over and let rise for 1 hour. Roll out and cut for biscuits. Let rise for another hour. Bake at 400°F. until golden brown.

Southern Raised Biscuits

4 cups sifted all-purpose flour ~ 2 teaspoons baking powder
4 cups sifted all-purpose flour ~ 1 teaspoon salt
1 package active dry yeast ~ 2 Tablespoons sugar
½ cup warm water ~ 1 cup buttermilk
½ cup shortening ~ 2 Tablespoons butter

This recipe isn't nearly as sweet as Mississippi River Biscuits but some people prefer the fluffier texture and lighter color of this recipe. Prepare as above.

Baby Biscuits may be just the right size for the youngsters or finicky eaters in your family. The recipe produces an air-light little biscuit, not traditional Southern, but perfect for those who prefer lighter fare.

Baby Biscuits

1 package yeast ~ 1 teaspoon salt
3 Tablespoons warm water ~ ¼ cup sugar
5 cups all-purpose flour ~ 1 cup shortening
1 teaspoon baking soda ~ 2 cups buttermilk
3 teaspoons baking powder

Dissolve yeast in warm water with a pinch of the sugar and let stand for 10 minutes, or until foamy. Mix dry ingredients together. Rub shortening into dry mix with fingers until the size of peas. Add yeast to buttermilk. Stir buttermilk mixture into flour just until all flour is moistened. Cough will be very sticky. Cover with plastic wrap and refrigerate overnight before using. In the morning preheat oven to 425°F. Place about 1 cup of flour on a piece of wax paper. Dust hands with flour, pinch off a piece of dough the size of a small egg, roll lightly in hands to shape. Place with sides touching on a lightly greased baking sheet. Bake for 10-15 minutes or until brown.

Southerners do eat other things for breakfast besides biscuits and grits though I wonder sometimes why we bother. The following recipes represent some of the other breakfast favorites that you'll find in the Deep South. They range from the very sweet French Toast and homemade Donuts to the more healthy homemade Watermelon Preserves. I finish this chapter with recipes for those Southern favorites along with the South's favorite sausage and egg recipe.

We rarely ate meat or eggs growing up in the rural South. Regardless, many of those foods are today considered "traditional" breakfast entrees. Similarly, I can't remember ever having anything resembling today's packaged cereals. What we ate we first grew! Therefore I leave most of those recipes for generic cookbook authors. Sausage and Egg Casserole, however, is truly Southern.

Sausage & Egg Casserole

8 ounces sausage, broken up, cooked & drained
½ pound sharp cheese, grated ~ 7 slices bread, torn up
¼ pound butter, melted ~ 2 teaspoons dry mustard
5 eggs, beaten ~ 2 teaspoons salt ~ 2 cups milk

Beat together the dry mustard, beaten eggs, salt and milk. In a large, shallow casserole put bread on bottom, then melted butter and sausage. Pour egg mixture over top; cover and refrigerate overnight. Bake at 350°F. until cheese melts and it is light brown around the edges, usually about 30-45 minutes.

Kid's Favorite French Toast

3 or 4 eggs ~ 4 cups milk
⅛ cup sugar ~ 1 teaspoon cinnamon ~ Texas toast bread
2 sticks butter or margarine ~ powdered sugar or syrup

Heat butter in large skillet. Mix sugar and cinnamon. Add eggs and milk to make batter. Dip slices of bread in batter. Fry battered bread until browned on both sides. Sprinkle with powdered sugar or syrup.

The remainder of the breakfast recipes are arranged in no particular order. They are simply the best of the Southern best.

Homemade Donuts

1 can prepared biscuits ~ Cinnamon
Sugar, granulated or powered ~ Deep fat, hot

Separate biscuits. Cut hole in center. Fry in hot grease, turning once. Sprinkle with mixture of cinnamon and sugar.

Chocolate Pancakes

2 cups self-rising flour ~ 2 teaspoons sugar
3 teaspoons cocoa ~ 2 eggs, well beaten
4 teaspoons melted shortening ~ 1¾ cups milk

Sift together the flour, sugar and cocoa; add eggs, milk and shortening and mix well. Drop by spoonfuls on slightly greased griddle. Serve hot with butter and syrup.

Apple Raisin Bars

1½ cups melted butter ~ 2 cups brown sugar
4 cups flour ~ 2 teaspoons soda
1½ cups rolled oats ~ 2 teaspoons vanilla
Filling:
3 cups apple sauce
2 cups raisins (soak overnight in fruit juice and drain)
1 cup brown sugar ~ 1 teaspoon lemon juice

Blend melted butter and sugar together. Stir in dry ingredients. Put
½ of the crumb mixture into greased baking pan. Press firmly. Mix
filling ingredients and spread over crumb mixture. Cover with
remaining crumb mixture. Bake at 350°F. for 30 minutes. Cut in
squares.

Watermelon Rind Preserves

Rind from 1 watermelon
2 Tablespoons pickling lime ~ Sugar ~ Salt
1 Lemon, sliced ~ 1 teaspoon cloves
1 teaspoon allspice ~ 2 sticks cinnamon
1 ounce brandy extract
Red or green food coloring (optional)

Peel rind, being careful to cut off all rind and all green parts. Cut
into small pieces and add enough water to cover. Add pickling lime
and let stand 3 to 4 hours. Drain and wash well. Weight the rind
and add an equal amount of sugar (1 pound sugar for 1 pound
rind). Almost cover with water. To each gallon of rind, add 1
teaspoon salt and 1 sliced lemon. Tie in a cheesecloth cloves,
allspice and cinnamon and add to the rind mixture. Cook until it
makes a thick syrup. Remove spices in cheesecloth. Add brandy
extract. Put into jars and add coloring as desired. Then seal. Ten
pounds of watermelon yields about 5 pints.

Finally a Southern breakfast wouldn't be complete without Hoe Cakes and Johnny Cakes. There's lots of stories about how these got their name; none of them reliable. We just know they're irresistible.

Hoe Cakes

2 Tablespoons Shortening ~ ¼ teaspoon baking soda
1½ cups self-rising cornmeal ~ 1 egg, slightly beaten
1¼ cups low fat buttermilk

Combine cornmeal and baking soda in medium bowl. Add buttermilk, egg, and one Tablespoon melted shortening. Stir just until dry ingredients are moistened. Heat 1 Tablespoon shortening on medium-high heat in non-stick skillet. Pour ¼ cup batter into skillet for each hoe cake. Fry 1 to 2 minutes or until golden brown on each side. Drain on paper towels.

Johnny Cakes

1 egg ~ 1 cup all-purpose flour ~ ⅓ cup sugar
¾ cup cornmeal ~ ¼ cup butter flavored shortening
½ teaspoon salt ~ 1 cup sour milk ~ 1 teaspoon baking soda
18 teaspoons maple syrup, jam, or honey

Combine egg, sugar, and 1 Tablespoon plus 1 teaspoon butter flavored shortening in medium bowl. Stir in sour milk and baking soda. Add flour, cornmeal, and salt. Stir just until dry ingredients are moistened. Cover and let stand in a cool place for 30 minutes. Pour the remaining shortening on a griddle or in a large skillet. Heat on medium heat. Spoon Tablespoonfuls of batter onto griddle. Brown on one side then turn, and brown on the other side. Serve with syrup, jam, or honey.

Chapter 3
Dirt-water Dinners

Typical Fancy Dinner Place Setting

You'll quickly note that this dinner setting isn't for everyday. However, if you're having a luncheon or special guests for dinner this is the correct way to arrange your dinner table.

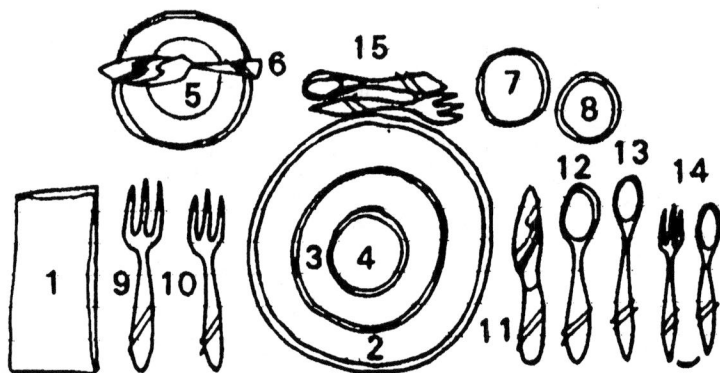

1. Napkin, folded across plate.   2. Plate
3. Liner plate for first course
4. Soup or seafood or fruit service
5. Bread-and-butter plate
6. Butter knife
7. Water glass or goblet
8. Wine goblet
9. Fork
10. Salad fork (place left of main course fork if salad is served first)
11. Knife
12. Soup spoon (used if soup is served)
13. Coffee or tea spoon (may be brought in with coffee service)
14. Seafood fork or fruit cocktail spoon (used when a first course of seafood or fruit replaces soup)
15. Dessert silver (may be brought in with dessert service)

American slang dictates that dinner is the evening meal. Not so in the South. Our dinner comes midday when the rest of the country is consuming "lunch." Southern dinners are light by demand rather than design. In the old days there was only an hour for lunch, midway between sunup and sundown. We didn't have clocks and watches like we do today. So when our shadows just about disappeared as the sun rose overhead and we thought we would pass out from the heat in the fields, we'd know that it was almost time for dinner.

Dinners haven't changed much in the Deep South. They consist largely of salads and light casseroles. One doesn't care to get overburdened with big meaty dinners as there remains a full day's work after dinner. My husband argues with me on this point. He says that on their farm dinner was the biggest meal of the day. It is possible that throughout the South each family's routine is different. Nevertheless, I remember fresh vegetables from the garden along with perhaps one huge biscuit. Today we enjoy a wider variety of dinners, but they remain airy and simple. Dinners take on a less significant role on Thursdays and Fridays when the entire community gathers at the Fish Camp for an early supper (see Chapter 4) while Sunday dinners can be elaborate, depending on who's coming after church.

Dinners are essentially a mid-day snack, chock full of carbohydrates to give us the energy to make it through the day. The following are some of the South's favorite mid-day meals. I've separated them by workdays, Fish Camp days, and Sundays as Southern weeks are divided up by important community and work functions.

Workdays in the South, Monday through Wednesday and Saturday, call for quick light and easy dinners. You can't go wrong with these choices.

Workday Dinners

Asparagus Casserole

2 Tablespoons margarine ~ 2 Tablespoons flour
1 cup milk ~ ¼ cup grated cheese
1 teaspoon onion juice ~ 3 eggs, boiled and chopped
1 Number 2 can asparagus ~ Salt and pepper to taste
1 cup butter bread crumbs

Make white sauce by melting margarine (or butter), adding flour, and whisking in milk. Cook and stir slowly until thickened. Add cheese, onion juice, salt, pepper, and eggs to sauce. Drain asparagus and add to mixture. Pour in casserole dish and top with butter bread crumbs. Bake in a 350°F. Oven for 20 minutes until crumbs are browned.

This Louisiana favorite is now a mainstay throughout the South. If your family is afraid of black beans, try snap beans or canned green beans. You won't get the same brothy texture but that can be overcome with a little flour added to the mix while its still hot.

Black Bean & Rice Salad

2 cups cooked rice, cooked in beef bouillon
2 cans black beans, drained ~ 4 stalks celery, diced small
2 carrots, diced small ~ Chopped chives
Feta cheese (if desired)
Dressing:
1 cup olive oil ~ 1 teaspoon garlic salt or powder
Salt and pepper ~ 1 teaspoon oregano
Vinegar to taste

Mix all ingredients, except cheese. Allow to sit in refrigerator for several hours. Sprinkle with cheese before serving.

If your tastes run hot, you'll love this next recipe from bayou country. It originated in South America as an entrada, or salad plate.

Burnin' Bayou Brunch Salad

5 pounds potatoes, any variety ~ Salt and pepper
3 hard boiled egg yolks ~ 1 cup oil
2 cups cheese (any variety) ~ ½ cup evaporated milk
1 Tablespoon lemon juice ~ ¼ cup onions, finely chopped
2 Tablespoons ground hot pepper ~ 5 hard-boiled eggs
1 hot pepper, cut in strips ~ 10 ripe Greek olives
Head of lettuce, any variety

Wash, remove eyes, and boil potatoes, skin on. While potatoes boil make sauce. In a blender, mix cheese, egg yolks, salt, pepper, and ground hot pepper. Add oil gradually, then lemon juice, milk, and onions. Slice potatoes in half and arrange on serving platter. Cover potatoes with sauce and garnish with olives, quartered boiled eggs, and hot pepper strips. Prepare on a bed of lettuce on individual serving plates.

Charleston Crisp Slaw

8 cups cabbage, shredded
2 cups carrots, diced ~ 1 green pepper, diced
½ cup chopped onion ~ ¾ cup cold water
⅔ cup salad oil ~ 1 envelope unflavored gelatin
¼ teaspoon pepper ~ 1½ teaspoons salt
2 teaspoons celery seed ~ ⅔ cup sugar ~ ⅔ cup vinegar

Mix vegetables, sprinkle with ½ cup cold water. Chill in refrigerator. Soften gelatine in ¼ cup cold water and set aside. Mix all other ingredients except salad oil and bring to boil in saucepan. Remove and stir in softened gelatine. Cool a little. Gradually beat in salad oil a little at a time. Cool till thickened. Drain vegetables and pour dressing over. Stir to mix well and chill. Stir before serving. Keeps about one week.

Chicken Pot Pie

Pie: 1 chicken, cooked in water, boned, broth reserved
1 8-ounce package frozen peas and carrots, parboiled 3 minutes
3 potatoes, peeled, cubed, and cooked
2 hard-boiled eggs, sliced (optional)
Dumplings made from pastry or dumpling dough

Sauce: ½ stick margarine ~ ⅓ cup flour
1 cup milk ~ 1 pint chicken broth
1 can Cream of Chicken Soup

Topping: 1 cup self-rising flour
1 stick margarine, melted ~ 1 cup milk

Sauce: Melt ½ stick margarine and stir together with flour. Whisk in 1 pint of reserved chicken broth and cook until thickened. Stir in soup and then milk. Pie: Place chicken, vegetables, optional eggs, and dumplings in a large baking dish, making two layers. Pour sauce on top, stirring in if necessary. Topping: Mix together flour melted stick of margarine and milk. Spoon or pour on top of pie. Bake at 375°F. For 40-45 minutes until topping is golden brown.

Collard Greens and Ham

1 ½ pounds collard leaves ~ 1 teaspoon sugar
¾ pound ham hock ~ ¼ teaspoon cayenne pepper
½ teaspoon salt ~ 2 quarts water

wash leaves in several changes of water. Break in to small pieces and add ham and seasonings. Cover with 2 quarts of water and boil until tender. Simmer over low heat for about 1 hour. Serve with vinegar.

Cranberries

Cranberries have been an American favorite since the first Thanksgiving. In the South these tart, bright red native berries are hand-picked from the swampy low-lands where they are indigenous. High-bush blueberries are now much more abundant in the South than any other kind of berry. They substitute nicely in the following dinner recipes.

Cranberry Salad

2 cups cranberry juice ~ 2 boxes lemon Jell-O
fruit and/or nuts as desired

Heat cranberry juice to mix with Jell-O. Add any kind of fruit or nuts desired.

Cranberry-Sweet Potato Casserole

4 large yams (about 2½ pounds) ~ ¼ cup brown sugar
3 Tablespoons butter ~ 1 cup fresh cranberries
½ cup orange juice ~ ½ cup chopped pecans
½ teaspoon cinnamon

Cook yams in microwave; cool, peel, and cut crosswise into ½-inch slices. Place half of the yams in a large casserole. Sprinkle with half of the brown sugar and half of the cranberries. Dot with half of the margarine. Layer with the remaining yams, brown sugar, cranberries, and margarine. Pour in orange juice. Cover and bake in a preheated 350°F. oven for 40 minutes. Sprinkle with pecans and cinnamon. Bake uncovered another 15 minutes.

Eggplant

One of the South's favorite "vegetables" is actually not a vegetable at all. It's the eggplant which is a berry belonging to the nightshade family that includes tomatoes and potatoes. Eggplant range in color from white to rich purple and derive their names from their egg-shaped fruit. These berries are a great source of fiber, are filling and low in calories. Great for a workday casserole.

Eggplant Casserole

2 large eggplant ~ 2 beaten eggs
¾ cup soft bread crumbs ~ 2 Tablespoons butter
2 teaspoons grated onion ~ 2 Tablespoons all-purpose flour
2 Tablespoons catsup ~ ¾ cup milk
1 teaspoon salt ~ 1 cup cubed Cheddar cheese
Dash of Worcestershire Sauce

Boil peeled and sliced eggplant in water until well done. Drain, mash, and mix with bread crumbs, onion, catsup, salt, pepper, Worcestershire sauce and eggs. Melt butter; stir in flour then add milk and cook until mixture thickens. Add to eggplant mixture. Stir in cheese. Place in buttered casserole. Bake at 350°F. For 30-40 minutes. Eggplant should be browned slightly and cheese well melted before removing from the oven.

Eggplant Stew

3 large potatoes ~ 1 unpeeled eggplant, trimmed
2 bell peppers (green or red) ~ 2 cloves garlic, minced
1 can crushed tomatoes ~ ¼ cup vegetable oil

Cut potatoes, eggplant, and trimmed and seeded peppers into 1-inch pieces. In a large pot combine all of the ingredients. Season to taste. Simmer on low until tender about 25 minutes.

Eggplant Zipporah Roast

1 large eggplant, cut into 1-inch cubes
1 large onion, cut into 1-inch cubes
½ 10-ounce package salad spinach, chopped
1 cup shredded mozzarella cheese
½ pound lean ground beef ~ 2 Tablespoons vegetable oil
1 jar tomato and basil sauce ~ 8 ounces ziti or rotini, cooked

Spread eggplant and onion on a large baking pan. Drizzle with oil. Roast at 450°F. For 20 minutes. Add ground beef and cook another 10 minutes. Toss eggplant with spinach, cooked pasta, and sauce. Sprinkle cheese on top. Reduce heat to 375°F. And bake, covered, for 20 minutes or until bubbly.

Eggplant Zucchini Spaghetti

3 Tablespoons vegetable oil ~ 3 cloves garlic, minced
1 small eggplant, peeled and cubed ~ 1 small zucchini, cubed
1 can (28-ounces) tomatoes ~ 6 ounces bacon
1 box (16-ounces) spaghetti

Cook bacon and cut into ½-inch strips. Set aside. Cook and drain pasta. Set aside. Heal oil in a large skillet. Add garlic, zucchini, eggplant and bacon. Sauté on medium for 5 minutes. Add tomatoes and simmer for about 5 minutes. Add cooked pasta. Season to taste. Toss to heat throughout.

Five-Cup Salad

1 cup miniature marshmallows ~ 1 cup sour cream
1 can mandarin oranges, cut up ~ ⅔ cup flake coconut
1 cup crushed pineapple

Mix well and chill. Dress this recipe up with maraschino cherries, nuts, and raisins according to your family's particular tastes.

Potatoes

Potatoes show up throughout this cookbook. They have always been a favored part of Southern cooking. A member of the nightshade family of plants, potatoes are cousins of peppers, tomatoes, and eggplants. Potatoes are fat free and provides lots of potassium, vitamin C, and fiber. They're also an excellent source of carbohydrates, just what you need to kick start the second half of the Southern day!

Potato Salad, Southern Style

My family loves fresh hot potato salad. I think it may be the only recipe that all three of my boys know how to make themselves. It is best hot but will keep for days in the refrigerator. This one is definitely a meal in itself.

5 pounds red potatoes
1 red medium onion, finely chopped
8-10 eggs, hard-boiled, finely chopped
1 teaspoon prepared mustard
Seasoned salt ~ 3 stalks celery, chopped fine (optional)
Mayonnaise or salad dressing

Cook whole red potatoes. Boil until tender; let set to slightly cool for 5 minutes. Rub off hot skins (it's easier when still hot). Let potatoes cool. Dice the potatoes when they reach room temperature. Mix the onion, optional celery, eggs and mustard. Add mix to diced potatoes, season salt and mayonnaise to taste. You'll surely have a particular one in the bunch. Leave out the celery and onions and substitute tangy kosher dills in their place. Salad dressing and extra mustard really zests up the basic recipe. Finally, if you don't have red potatoes on hand don't worry. Any potato will do. For a unique twist wash potatoes well and serve skin-on.

Potato Salad, Southern Style Hot

1 egg, slightly beaten ~ 1 teaspoon dry mustard
¼ cup sugar ~ 6 slices bacon ~ ½ cup vinegar
10 medium potatoes ~ ½ cup water ~ 2 onions

Chop bacon and fry until crisp. Combine bacon and grease with all other ingredients except onions and potatoes. Cook mixture until it thickens, stirring constantly. Chop potatoes and boil until tender then drain. Dice onions to potatoes. Pour sauce over onion-potato mixture and let cool for 5-10 minutes. Serve hot.

Potato Salad, Southern Style III
with Cottage Cheese

2 cups cooked, cubed potatoes ~ ½ cup mayonnaise
¼ cup sliced celery ~ ½ teaspoon salt
1 chopped bell pepper ~ ½ teaspoon dry mustard
2 Tablespoons chopped pimento
1½ teaspoon lemon juice ~ 1 Tablespoon minced onion
½ cup cottage cheese ~ 1 Tablespoon sweet pickle relish
Lettuce or other greens

Combine potatoes, celery, green pepper, pimento, onion and pickle relish; toss lightly. Chill. Combine mayonnaise, seasonings and lemon juice and add to potato mixture. Add cottage cheese stirring gently. Serve over lettuce.

The last potato salad recipe only feeds two hearty Southern appetites. You'll want to double it for an average size family. Often one or more of these ingredients is missing from the refrigerator when you got to throw together a quick dinner. Substitute sandwich mustard for dry mustard. Kosher dills, diced add a nice tangy and crunchy dimension to potato salad. If bell peppers are not available try dicing carrots into very small pieces just to add texture and color to the salad.

Spaghetti Salad was a staple during the lean times in the late 1930s and early 1940s in the rural South. I can remember when we had nothing but Spaghetti Salad and beans for weeks when a crop would fail or other unforseen financial hurdles would befall our family. It is still a good quick dish for dinner. I wouldn't recommend subsisting on it like we sometimes did, however.

Spaghetti Salad

1 small bottle creamy salad dressing
2 cups Italian dressing
1 pound cooked and drained spaghetti

Any vegetables you like (carrots, black olives, mushrooms, cucumbers and tomatoes are standard), chopped into bite-sized chunks.

Fresh squash is often abundant in the summer and fall in the South. Imported squash can now be found year round in supermarkets though it lacks the flavor of home grown. This recipe dresses up basic cooked squash.

Squash Casserole

2 cups cooked zucchini or yellow squash
1 can cream of chicken soup
¼ cup margarine ~ 1 cup sour cream
1 onion, chopped ~ 2 medium carrots, grated
½ package herb poultry seasoning
2-3 stalks celery, chopped (if desired)

Cook squash; drain. Grease casserole dish with margarine. Line with most of stuffing; mix all the other ingredients and pour into casserole. Top with rest of stuffing. Dot with margarine. Bake at 350°F. for 30 minutes.

Tennessee Twelve Day Salad is so named because it gets better every day you keep it, up to the twelfth anyway. This last workday dinner is best served with some sort of sausage or, preferably, corned beef.

Tennessee Twelve Day Salad

½ head cabbage ~ ½ cup vegetable oil
1 teaspoon celery seed ~ 1 medium onion
1 cup sugar ~ 1 cup white vinegar
½ green bell pepper ~ 1 teaspoon salt

Shred cabbage, onion and bell pepper. Add sugar to shredded mixture and set aside. Mix salt, vinegar, celery seed and oil in small pot; bring to a boil. Pour hot liquid over shredded mixture and stir thoroughly. Refrigerate in covered bowl at least 12 hours before serving. Will keep for 12 days and gets better with age.

Fish Camp days require the lightest of dinners. The Fish Camp is a Southern tradition that is not familiar outside of the South. It isn't quite like it sounds. I know my grandkids had some idea that the "Camp" was set up on a lake and that you'd catch your own catfish for dinner. In reality Fish Camps are small restaurants, generally far off the beaten path that dot the landscape of the remaining rural areas of the South. They are generally family owned and operated and serve a limited menu consisting of catfish, hush puppies and other indisputably Southern edibles. The Fish Camp is a place to gather and hear the community news, mid-week. It gets really hopping around 4:00 p.m. on Thursday and Friday nights. My mama insists on getting there right at four, before the good seats are taken. It's always all-you-can-eat catfish. Some Camps offer other all-you-can eat suppers of shrimp, oysters, or other easily fried fare available locally and always fresh. On Fish Camp days dinner is kept light and bite-sized so there's plenty of room leftover for the all-you-can-eat catfish supper, later in the evening. Better yet, skip dinner to save room for a huge supper!

Sunday dinner calls for a more elaborate presentation, especially if company is planned. The preacher generally makes his rounds once or twice a year. As kids we looked forward to his visit more than any other day of the year, except perhaps Christmas, because we knew that there would be a wonderful gourmet spread prepared by our mother. She'd hoard and save to pull out all the stops when the preacher finally made his way back to our home. Try these **Sunday Dinner Entree** recipes as centerpieces for a more supper-like **Sunday dinner**.

Stuffed Bell Peppers

6 medium green bell peppers ~ ½ cup rice
1 pound ground beef ~ ⅓ cup chopped onion
2 cups tomato sauce ~ 1½ teaspoons salt
¼ teaspoon black pepper
2 teaspoons bacon drippings or butter

Remove tops and seeds from bell peppers; parboil 5 minutes; drain. Partially cook the rice in 1 cup water. (Do not overcook.) Brown onion and ground beef in bacon drippings. Mix ground beef and onions with the cooked rice and 1 cup tomato sauce. Stand peppers upright in covered baking dish; stuff with rice and beef mixture; pour 1 cup tomato sauce over stuffed peppers. Cover baking dish. Bake at 325°F. for 45 minutes, uncover and bake 15 minutes.

Bell Peppers

Peppers are an excellent source of Vitamin C; one medium bell pepper provides 130% of the daily allowance (more than a medium orange)!

Cabbage

A cruciferous vegetable, cabbage contains natural chemical compounds that may be helpful in the prevention of certain types of cancers. Beware! Red cabbage tastes similar to green, but can run and discolor other foods.

Stuffed Cabbage

1 large head cabbage ~ 2 pounds ground beef
¾ cup raw rice ~ 2 eggs ~ 1 large onion, finely chopped
½ teaspoon salt ~ ½ cup vinegar
½ cup brown sugar ~ 1 cup tomato sauce

Drop whole cabbage into boiling water in large sauce pan. Let stand about 5 minutes, until soft enough to separate the leaves. Drain and cool enough to handle. Cut out hard stem end and carefully remove leaves, being sure to keep them as whole as possible. Combine beef, rice, eggs, onion and salt; blend thoroughly. Place a teaspoon of the mixture in center of each cabbage leaf; roll leaf around meat and tuck in the ends. Place rolls close together in a large saucepan. Combine vinegar, sugar, tomato sauce and water to make just enough sauce to cover the rolls. Cover tightly; simmer over low heat 1 hour. Remove cover, cook about 15 minutes, until sauce is slightly thickened.

Sunday Dinner Entrees

The following recipes represent some other common Southern dinner fare. We didn't eat much chicken in the old days. I also can't ever remember eating pizza until I was in my 50s. Regardless, they're both a big part of the Southern diet today.

Biloxi Belle's Hot Chicken Salad

4 cups cooked chicken, cut up ~ 2 teaspoons lemon juice
¾ cup mayonnaise ~ 1 teaspoon salt
2 cups chopped celery ~ 4 hard-boiled eggs, chopped
¾ cup cream of chicken soup ~ 1 small onion, finely minced
1½ cups crushed potato chips ~ 1 cup grated cheddar cheese
⅔ cup toasted almonds

Combine all ingredients, except cheese, potato chips and almonds. Place in 13 x 9-inch baking dish. Top with cheese and almonds. Chill overnight. Just before cooking, top with potato chips. Bake at 400°F. for 20-25 minutes.

Chicken Casserole

1 can cheddar cheese soup ~ ½ cup milk
1 cup diced cooked chicken ~ 2 cups cooked noodles
1 teaspoon finely chopped parsley

Stir cheddar cheese soup in 1 ½ quart casserole dish until smooth; gradually add milk. Mix in remaining ingredients. Bake at 350°F. for 30 minutes.

Add green beans, mushrooms, squash, broccoli, or cheese as you like it. Just about anything can be added to a casserole to dress it up to match your family's tastes.

Fried rice is an uncommon dish that we often lived on during the roughest months in the early 1940s. Everyone's heard of it but few are familiar with how to make it, Southern style. This recipe is quick, unique and tasty. Perfect on the occasions when your Sunday dinner guests are a surprise. I've used the following recipe several times when unannounced guests arrived around dinner-time on a Sunday. I dress it up with whatever vegetables I have lying around. It's a throwback to the days when we often had nothing to eat *but* rice and eggs. The recipe takes less than 10 minutes to prepare and will certainly have your guests begging for a copy of your recipe card. If you don't have bell peppers add pimentos or even diced carrots; any kind of vegetable for color. It makes a nice entree around which **Sunday dinner** can be built.

Fried Rice

¼ cup plus ~ 2 teaspoons butter or margarine
2 eggs, beaten ~ ⅔ cup chopped green onions
⅔ cup chopped red bell pepper ~ 2⅔ cups cooked rice
⅔ cup water ~ ¼ cup soy sauce

Melt butter in a large skillet; add eggs and cook over medium heat until almost set. Stir in green onions, red pepper, and cooked rice; cook, stirring frequently, about 5 minutes or until lightly browned. Add water and soy sauce. Cook another 2 minutes.

Quiche

Quiche is a German dish, adopted by the French and imported throughout the South from the ports along the Mississippi River. The quiche, often called a quiche Lorraine, consists of a rich unsweetened custard baked in a pastry shell, often with other ingredients. Spinach quiche is a great variation for those wishing to go the extra mile to chop, drain, and cook spinach prior to using a recipe like the following. Most of us don't have the time and/or energy for all that work. This version from Missouri is my favorite.

Kansas City Quiche

1 unbaked 9-inch pastry crust ~ ¼ cup melted butter
2 cups half-and-half ~ 4 well-beaten eggs
½ cup crisp cut-up bacon (about ½ pound)
¾ cup grated Swiss or cheddar cheese
¼ teaspoon freshly-ground pepper

Bake crust at 450° F. for 10 to 12 minutes. Brush with butter and chill. Scald cream in double boiler. Slowly stir in eggs. When thoroughly combined, remove from heat. Stir in bacon, cheese and pepper. Pour into crust. Bake at 350°F. for 45 minutes, or until knife inserted in center comes out clean. Makes 6 servings.

Porcupine Balls

1 pound ground beef ~ ½ cup rice, uncooked
1 Bell pepper, chopped ~ 1 small onion, chopped
1 can condensed tomato soup ~ ¼ teaspoon pepper
1 cup water ~ 2 Tablespoons fat, melted ~ Salt to taste

Blend beef, rice, bell pepper, onion, salt, and pepper together thoroughly. Shape meat into balls about the size of a walnut. Arrange balls in a large, heavy skillet. Pour tomato soup, water, and melted fat over meat balls. Cook at high heat until steaming, reduce to lowest heat for 45 minutes. You can prepare Porcupine Balls in advance and store in the freezer. Make sauce and heat an hour before dinnertime.

Sweet Potato

Sweet Potato is the common name applied to a perennial, trailing herb of the morning glory family. The plant is native to tropical America and is widely cultivated in the South. For many it represents an important starchy staple food. We also have other "sweet potatoes" called manroot or man-of-the-earth. Don't try making a dinner of those. They are not recommended for human consumption, rather for their esthetic value. One more note on the sweet potato: In the South the correct terminology is "yam." If they don't know what a **sweet potato** is they'll surely know a yam!

I could write a whole book filled with sweet potato recipes. I remember times when we survived largely on sweet potatoes and rice. They've lost some favor in modern society because of their less-than-sweet flavor and mushy texture. Those "flaws" can quickly be overcome with some sugar and refrigeration. Sweet potatoes are available year round and I can't think of an occasion when they wouldn't add color and panache to a meal. Forget the hot sweet potato recipes you see in the movies about the South. We really don't eat marshmallows on everything. Try this casserole at your next big **Sunday dinner**. They'll never know that the main ingredient is the lowly yam.

Sweet Potato Casserole

3 cups cooked sweet potatoes ~ 1 cup sugar
2 eggs ~ ½ cup milk ~ ½ cup melted butter
1 teaspoon vanilla ~ 1 teaspoon cinnamon
1 teaspoon nutmeg

Topping: 1 cup brown sugar ~ ⅓ cup flour
⅓ cup melted butter ~ ½ cup chopped pecans

Mix together potatoes, sugar, eggs, milk and butter. Stir in vanilla, cinnamon and nutmeg. Put in greased casserole dish.
Topping: Mix together brown sugar, flour, melted butter and pecans. Sprinkle on top of potato mixture. Bake at 350°F. for 30 minutes or until top is brown.

Sweet Potato & Rice Crunch

1 cup cooked rice ~ 1 cup sugar ~ ½ teaspoon salt
2 eggs, beaten ~ ½ cup milk ~ ½ teaspoon vanilla
½ stick butter ~ 3 cups cooked sweet potatoes, mashed

Mix rice, potatoes, sugar, salt, eggs, softened butter, milk, and vanilla. Pour into a 2-quart casserole. Add the following topping:

Topping: ½ cup Rice Krispies ~ ⅓ stick butter
½ cup chopped pecans ~ ⅓ cup plain flour
1 cup brown sugar

Combine brown sugar and flour, then add melted butter and mix. Add nuts and Rice Krispies. Spread topping over sweet potato mixture. Bake at 350°F. For 35 minutes. Dress up the finished dish with ice cream, whipped cream or frozen whipped topping to create a pudding-like concoction.

Vegetable Bake

10 ounce frozen or fresh chopped broccoli, cooked and drained
2 eggs, beaten ~ 2 cups cream-style corn
1 cup sour cream ~ 1 small box cornmeal mix
¼ butter or margarine, melted

Combine all ingredients together in a large bowl. Pour into a 9 x 13-inch aluminum or glass pan. Cook in preheated oven at 350°F. for one hour. Substitute any combination of vegetable that you like. This recipe dresses-up nicely with mushrooms and broccoli, peas and cream-style corn, carrots and cauliflower or any other combination you can think of. Add 1 cup of water if your vegetables aren't as "wet" as the cream-style corn called for in the original version of the dish.

Vidalia Onions

Vidalia onions have grown in popularity as an appetizer in trendy themed restaurant chains in recent years; they're nothing new to true Southerners! Vidalia onions are a Peidmont favorite. Nicknamed the "Sweetie," the Vidalia gets its flavor from the sandy, low sulfur soil and temperate climate found in southeast Georgia's Vidalia onion country. Often served raw, the Vadialia is very sweet, crisp, and juicy with just a hint of heat. Try these age-old Southern Georgia speciality when the Vidalias are in season, mid-April through August.

Vidalia Onions, Scalloped

3 large Vidalia onions, cleaned, peeled, and sliced
½ teaspoon salt ~ ¼ cup margarine ~ 1 cup milk
2 cups grated American cheese

Slice onions and separate into rings. Place in a 1½-quart casserole. Melt margarine and blend in flour. Slowly stir in milk and cook until thickened. Stir in salt and grated cheese. Pour over onions. Bake uncovered for 1 hour at 375° F.

Vidalia Onions Stuffed with Chicken Liver

2 pounds chicken liver, chopped ~ Milk
Flour ~ 6 large Vidalia onions
½ cup canned condensed mushroom soup
1 cup buttered bread crumbs ~ Oil

Steam onions for about ½ hour or until tender. Turn upside down to cool and drain. Remove a part of the center and fill the cavity with liver stuffing. Stand in a deep baking dish. Pour the mushroom soup in the bottom of the dish. Sprinkle with buttered bread crumbs. Cover the dish and bake at 350°F. until onions are soft. Uncover last 10 minutes so crumbs will brown nicely.

Liver stuffing: Dip chicken livers in milk and then in a mixture of flour and seasonings to taste. A little salt and pepper at the very least will perk up the flavor. For a nice bite add creole salt seasoning mix to the flour. Fry in oil until well done. Drain, cool, and stuff in center of onions.

This book is dedicated to my sister Marion. One of her many talents was cooking. Of all her unique recipes her Goulash is best remembered by me and my boys. This seemed as good a place as any to include this cherished recipe. She'd make such a big pot of it that we'd have to eat it for breakfast, lunch, *and* supper!

Marion's Goulash

3 pounds ground chuck ~ 2 large onions, chopped
6 potatoes peeled, and cubed, large ~ 1 can whole corn
2 cans green beans ~ 2 large cans whole tomatoes
1 8-ounce can tomato sauce ~ Seasonings to taste

Brown meat and onion in a large skillet or pot. Drain meat then add tomatoes and sauce. Cook over medium heat for 20 minutes. Add potatoes, corn, and green beans. Cook, bubbling, stirring every few minutes, for 30 minutes. Add salt, pepper, and other spices to taste. Other veggies may be added as desired. This dish is especially good in fall and winter. Serve with hot bread, rolls, or biscuits for a complete meal.

My sister, who incidentally lived her latter years in the very Southern Mobile, Alabama, would make this Louisiana Style. She'd add enough Creole seasoning and tabasco to make it almost inedible. She also liked to add red beans on the second and third days. That is to say the second and third day after the original dish was made. She'd always say that it got better and better with age. We thought that it got better *and* hotter and hotter.

Chapter 4
Friday at the Fish Camp

I don't know when the Fish Camp became a Southern institution but it has been around for the enjoyment of many generations of hungry Southerners. The "camps" are really homemade restaurants strewn throughout the Southern backwoods. We've tried many and find that the standard menu is similar; catfish fillets, hush puppies, slaw, and homemade iced tea. Some offer some more elaborate edibles including shrimp, chicken, steak, venison and other wild game available in a particular locality. The appetizers range from Vidalia onions, prepared with a variety of sauces and modes of cooking, to homemade saltines and slaw. Desserts consist of homemade pies, cakes, and ice cream which alone draw some sweet-toothed natives. No matter what extras are on the menu, the fish is always fresh, fried, and it's always all-you-can-eat. You won't find any salad bars or trendy music in Fish Camps. Everyone is there to hear the mid-week gossip and to gorge on the wonderfully fresh fried and baked delights. I've divided Fish Camp recipes into appetizers, catfish, and a few special drinks. These are some recipes that will never truly leave the South!

Appetizers and Side Dishes

Appetizers and side dishes are organized alphabetically, not necessarily according to my own personal favorites. I'd have a hard time choosing which Fish Camp appetizer I liked best, though Hush Puppies are certainly the second item that comes to mind when I think about an authentic Southern catfish dinner, the catfish being first, of course. Pickled Okra, Mayonnaise Bread, and Boiled Peanuts are other, uniquely Southern, appetizer favorites of mine. Kids often prefer various onion dishes, Cheese Sticks, and Potato Wedgies which are less traditional but are standard menu fare in the South. I've chosen the top 12 appetizers from an informal sampling of Fish Camps across the South. Its a tough job but. . .

Appalachian Cole Slaw

4-5 pounds cabbage ~ 2 medium onions
1 red bell pepper ~ 1 green bell pepper
1 cup sugar ~ 1 teaspoon salt
¾ cup cider vinegar ~ ¾ cup vegetable oil
1 teaspoon prepared mustard ~2 teaspoons celery seed
Dash of garlic powder

Shred cabbage using sharp knife. Chop onions and peppers. Mix together in large bowl. Sprinkle with half the sugar and set aside. Mix remaining sugar, salt, vinegar, oil, mustard, celery seed and garlic powder. Bring to a full boil; pour over cabbage mixture. Mix well. Let sit at least 6 hour before serving. Keeps for several days in refrigerator. Served with a jumbo buttermilk biscuit (See Breakfast Biscuit recipes).

Broccoli Cornbread

1 box cornbread mix ~ 2 eggs
1 cup milk ~ 1 cup chopped onions
2 cups grated cheese
1 cup frozen chopped broccoli ~ 1 stick margarine

Cook broccoli according to directions on box and drain. Mix all other ingredients except margarine. Melt ½ of margarine and put in baking dish. Mix other ½ of margarine with the ingredients. Bake at 400°F. for 30 minutes.

Hush Puppies

Hush Puppies are a true Southern tradition. There are dozens of ways to prepare them ranging from the basic recipe provided here to the super-extravagant varieties found in the South's finest restaurants. Dress up the plain recipe by adding instant beef flavoring.

Hush Puppies, Plain

1 teaspoon enriched flour ~ 2 cups cornmeal
6 Tablespoons chopped onion ~ 1 egg
1 Tablespoon salt ~ 1 cup buttermilk
1 teaspoon baking powder ~ ½ teaspoon soda

Mix all dry ingredients; add chopped onion, then milk and egg. Drop by spoonfuls into deep fat. Cook until brown. When done, they will float. Put on brown paper to drain.

Mayonnaise Bread, Pickled Okra, Boiled Peanuts, Baked Vidalia Onions, and Yam Cakes are all appetizers that you'll find nowhere else in the world but in the South's best Fish Camps. You'll be amazed at how simple it is to prepare these four Southern favorites.

Mayonnaise Bread

1 cup self-rising flour ~ 1 cup milk
3 Tablespoons mayonnaise

Blend all ingredients together well. Drop by Tablespoonsful into a greased muffin pan. Bake at 350° F. for 20 minutes or until golden brown.

Okra

Okra is one of the South's favorite vegetables. The following pickled recipe can trace its roots back to Ethiopian slaves who brought the vegetable to the South. Okra's green pods have a rigid skin and a tapered, oblong shape. When cooked, okra gives off a sticky juice that will thicken any liquid to which it is added making it a favored ingredient for creole gumbo. The flavor of okra falls somewhere between that of eggplant and asparagus. It is low calorie, low in sodium and cholesterol and fat free.

Okra, Pickled

8 cups small okra ~ 1 cup cider vinegar
¼ cup water ~ 2 Tablespoons salt
2 teaspoons dill seed ~ 4 cloves garlic
2 pods hot pepper

Sterilize 2 pint jars. Wash okra. Bring water, vinegar and salt to a boil. Pack okra in jars. To each add 1 tablespoon of dill seed, 2 garlic cloves and 1 hot pepper. Pour boiling liquid into jar, covering okra. Remove air bubbles, adjust lids and process in water bath for 5 minutes. Wait 1 month before using. Chill for crispness.

Anyone who has taken a road trip through the South has seen the road side stands selling "goobers" or peanuts that have been boiled in a brine solution. Here's the recipe so you can make them at home.

Peanuts, Boiled

1 pound fresh, raw, peanuts in shells
10 ounces salt ~ 1 gallon water

Wash in shell freshly harvested raw peanuts in cool water. Combine all ingredients and bring to boil. Simmer for 1 hour or until peanuts are soft.

Vidalia Onions, Baked

1 Vidalia onion per person
(substitute any sweet, yellow onion as available, peeled)
1 Tablespoon butter per ~ Onion salt and pepper

Preheat oven to 350°F. Place each onion on a square of heavy-duty aluminum foil. Add butter, season generously, and wrap tightly. Bake for 1 hour. Onions may also be cooked, wrapped in foil, on a hot grill for 30 to 45 minutes, or until soft. Turn frequently.

Yam Cake

½ cup vegetable oil ~ 2 cups sugar ~ 4 eggs
2 cups flour, sifted ~ 2 Tablespoons baking powder
1 tablespoon soda ~ 2 Tablespoons cinnamon
3 cups raw yams, grated ~ 1 cup pecans, finely chopped
1 box 10x powdered sugar ~ 1 cup orange juice ~ Salt

Preheat oven to 325° F. Combine oil and sugar and mix well. Sift together remaining dry ingredients. Add to sugar and oil mixture, alternating with eggs, added one at a time. Add grated yams and mix well. Stir in pecans and pour into a greased and floured bunt pan. Bake for 1 hour and 10 minutes. Cool in upright pan. Make a glaze of powdered sugar and orange juice. Douse almost cool cake with glaze.

Catfish

Flounder, shrimp, and steak recipes are common in American cookbooks; catfish recipes are harder to find. Since most Fish Camps specialize in catfish we're including only catfish recipes here, gathered from throughout the south. **Filleted Fried Catfish is a** Southern tradition. These are the basic recipe that you'll find throughout the Southeast United States.

Basic Fried Catfish

Catfish fillets ~ Yellow corn meal
Salt and Pepper ~ Oil

Put catfish fillets in cold water. Season corn meal with salt and pepper. Dredge fillets in corn meal and coat thoroughly. Fry in hot oil, turning fish once. Drain on paper towels or brown bags.

Citified Catfish is only slightly different from the basic recipe. The cornmeal sticks to the fillets somewhat better with this variation of the basic recipe.

Citified Filleted Fried Catfish

¾ cup yellow cornmeal ~ ¼ cup flour
2 teaspoons salt ~ 1 teaspoon cayenne pepper
¼ teaspoon garlic powder ~ 4 catfish fillets
vegetable oil ~ 2 eggs ~ Milk

Combine cornmeal, flour, salt, pepper, and garlic powder. Coat catfish with mixture. Whip eggs with about 1 cup of milk. Dunk fillets in milk/egg mixture then back into cornmeal mixture. Fry in hot oil heated to about 350° F. Add catfish in a single layer, and fry until golden brown, about 5-6 minutes. Remove and drain on paper towel or brown paper bags. This recipe makes four single servings.

Kids love **Breaded Catfish Strips** which are really just fillets sauteed in a slightly richer batter mixture.

Breaded Catfish Strips

2 pounds catfish fillets ~ 1 cup buttermilk
1 teaspoon salt ~ ½ teaspoon pepper
1 cup cornmeal ~ 1 egg, beaten with buttermilk
1 cup shortening ~ Lemon wedges
Sliced onion

Coat fillets with buttermilk. Season with salt and pepper. Dip fillets into corn meal, then dip into egg mixture and back into corn meal. Sauté in hot shortening for about 12 minutes or until golden brown, turning once or twice. Garnish with lemon wedges and sliced onion.

If your family doesn't like cornmeal you might want to try this almost fried catfish dish.

Oven-Fried Catfish Fillets

1 pound catfish fillets ~ ¼ cup mayonnaise
Bread crumbs ~ Paprika
½ teaspoon salt ~ ¼ teaspoon pepper
Lemon wedges

Thinly coat fish fillets with mayonnaise; dredge each in bread crumbs. Arrange in a greased 13 x 9 x 2-inch baking pan; sprinkle fillets with seasonings. Bake at 450°F. for 12 minutes or until fish flakes with a fork. Garnish fillets with lemon wedges.

The next best thing to Fried Catfish is Broiled Catfish. The following recipe is a wonderful variation for those who can't eat fried foods. It calls for herbs that may be hard to find in your area. Substitute your favorite herbs or any pre-mixed herb varieties.

Broiled Catfish with Herbs

1 Tablespoon margarine ~ 1 pound catfish fillets
3 teaspoons dried dill ~ ¼ teaspoon fine herbs
1 Tablespoon fresh parsley ~ 3 teaspoons fennel seed
1½ teaspoons chopped tarragon ~ 1½ teaspoons pepper
3 teaspoons dried dill

Combine fennel seed, tarragon, pepper, and dill. Set aside. Combine all sauce ingredients in sauce pan (margarine, herbs, and parsley); heat slowly until margarine is melted. Place catfish fillets on broiler pan and brush with sauce. Broil about 4 minutes, flip fillets and broil another 4 minutes or until fish flakes when tested with a fork. Sprinkle with fennel/tarragon/dill mixture. This recipe works equally well on an outdoor grill.

Root beer battered fish is a speciality found in a few fish camps in Southern Mississippi. The differences are obvious. This recipe doesn't call for corn meal and it makes a thicker batter on the fillets. It is an extremely easy recipe you can try at home, if you're not fortunate enough to live close to a camp that serves this delicious catfish recipe. Try substituting fresh sassafras tea in place of the root beer for another unique concoction.

Root Beer Battered Catfish

2 pounds catfish, fresh or thawed frozen
2 eggs, separated ~ ½ cup root beer
1 cup milk ~ 1 cup flour
½ teaspoon seasoned salt ~ ¼ teaspoon pepper

Cut fish into pieces about 3 x 1-inch. Place on paper towels to dry. Beat egg yolks until thick and light. Blend in root beer, milk, flour, and seasonings. Mix until smooth. Beat egg whites stiff, but not dry; fold into mixture. Dunk filets into batter a few pieces at a time. Deep fry until done.

Crunchy Potato Catfish

1 cup instant mashed potatoes ~ 1 egg, slightly beaten
1 Tablespoon lemon juice ~ 1 teaspoon salt
⅛ teaspoon pepper ~ 2 pounds catfish fillets
¼ to ½ cup shortening
2 Tablespoons sesame seeds (or poppy seeds)

Combine instant mashed potatoes and sesame seeds, mixing well. Set aside. Combine egg, lemon juice, salt, and pepper; mix well. Dip fish in egg mixture and then flour in potato mixture. Melt shortening in a large skillet over medium heat. Fry fish in shortening until golden brown. Makes about 5 servings. The substitution of mashed potatoes for corn meal results in an interesting, rich looking batter. They'll think this took hours!

The next 9 recipes represent some fancier (some not) and more time-consuming catfish recipes that I'm sure you'll love. I've included all the favorites from the very challenging Catfish Parmesan to the simple Catfish Kabobs.

Catfish Parmesan

⅔ cup grated Parmesan cheese ~ ¼ cup all-purpose flour
½ teaspoon salt ~ ½ teaspoon pepper
1 teaspoon paprika ~ 1 egg, beaten
¼ cup milk ~ 1 pound catfish fillets
¼ cup margarine, melted ~ ⅓ cup sliced almonds

Combine cheese, flour, salt, pepper, and paprika. Combine egg and milk and whip. Dip fillets in egg mixture then dredge in flour mixture. Arrange coated fillets in a lightly greased baking dish measuring 13 by 9 by 2-inches then drizzle with butter. Sprinkle almonds on top of the battered and buttered fillets. Bake at 350° F. for 35 to 40 minutes or until fish flakes easily when forked.

Cajun Catfish

1½ to 2 pounds catfish ~ 4 Tablespoons hot sauce
4 Tablespoons mustard ~ Yellow corn meal

Cut catfish into small thin pieces. Mix hot sauce with mustard. Dip strips into hot sauce mixture; let marinate 2 to 4 hours. Dip marinated catfish in corn meal; fry in hot oil until brown.

Quick & Easy Texas Catfish

4 catfish fillets ~ 1 16-ounce jar Picante sauce
6-8 ounces Monterey Jack cheese, grated

Place catfish in microwaveable dish. Microwave (vented) for 10 minutes. Add Picante and cheese and cook another 2 minutes.

Honey Bar-B-Qued Catfish

1 pound filleted catfish ~ 3 Tablespoons butter
2 Tablespoons cornstarch or flour ~ 1 cup tomato catsup
2 Tablespoons Worcestershire sauce ~ 1 Tablespoon honey
1 Tablespoon pineapple preserves ~ Red onion rings
⅛ teaspoon hot pepper sauce ~ Lemon wedges
⅛ teaspoon garlic juice ~ 4 slices pineapple
4 cups white whole kernel corn ~ 2 Tablespoons lemon juice
2 Tablespoons butter, melted ~ 3 Tablespoons green onion

Score fish on both sides, diamond shaped, making cuts about 1-inch apart. Dust fish with cornstarch. Place fish on a well greased broiler pan. Finely chop green onions and combine in a saucepan with other ingredients except pineapple, corn, melted butter, onion rings and lemon wedges. Bring mixture to a boil, stirring constantly; simmer for 10 minutes. Brush fish generously with sauce, being sure sauce gets into scored sections. Broil approximately 6-inches from source of heat for 4 minutes. Turn fish and brush liberally with sauce. Place pineapple on broiler pan with fish. Broil 4 additional minutes or until fish flakes easily with a fork and pineapple is slightly browned. Heat corn while fish is broiling. Drain liquid from corn and stir in melted butter. Spread corn over bottom of a warm shallow platter, building up sides slightly. Line the catfish down the center, flanking with pineapple slices on either end. Spoon the remaining heated sauce over the catfish only. Garnish with onion rings and lemon.

Catfish Kabob

2 pounds catfish fillets ~ 1 cup boiling water
12 small white onions, peeled ~ 18 large mushroom caps
12 large stuffed Spanish olives ~ 12 cherry tomatoes
½ cup vegetable oil½ cup teriyaki or soy sauce
½ cup onion, finely chopped ~ ⅓ cup lemon juice
1 Tablespoon sugar ~ 20 pecan halves
2 cloves garlic, peeled ~ ¼ teaspoon hot pepper sauce
½ teaspoon white pepper ~ 3 cups cooked rice
Parsley sprigs (for garnish) ~ Cherry tomatoes (for garnish)
6 wooden kabob skewers
Red and green pickled cherry peppers
2 Tablespoons whole coriander seed or caraway seed
2 cups herb seasoned croutons, crushed into crumbs

Cut fish into 1-inch pieces. Parboil white onions in water for 5 minutes, drain. In a large shallow dish, combine fish, white onions, mushroom caps, tomatoes and olives. Place croutons in a shallow dish. Place oil, teriyaki sauce, chopped onion, lemon juice, seed, sugar, pecans, garlic, pepper, and hot pepper sauce in blender or processor. Blend until onion and nuts are finely chopped and marinade is well blended. Pour marinade over fish and vegetables, stirring well to coat all pieces. Cover and marinate in refrigerator for 1 hour, stirring once during the marinating process. Drain; reserve marinade. Roll fish pieces in crumbs. Thread fish and vegetables, alternating, on 6 skewers approximately 16 inches long. Place on a greased broiler pan. Broil 9 or 10 inches from source of heat for 8 to 10 minutes. Turn kabob, baste with marinade and continue to cook another 8 to 10 minutes or until fish flakes easily with a fork. About 1 minute before cooking time is finished, brush any remaining marinade over kabob. Serve kabob over cooked rice. Garnish with parsley, cherry tomatoes and pickled cherry peppers. Makes 6 servings. Just a note of warning, **Catfish Kabobs** take a bit of preparation and some time but they are always a real hit!

Catfish Lafitte

Catfish batter:
2 eggs ~ 1 cup milk
2 cups all-purpose flour ~ 2 teaspoons salt
1 teaspoon cayenne pepper ~ 4 catfish fillets
Sauce:
3 Tablespoons butter, melted ~ 12 shrimp, shelled/deveined
½ teaspoon chopped garlic ~ 12 3-inch by ¼-inch ham strips
1 Tablespoon dry vermouth ~ ½ cup heavy cream
Dash cayenne pepper ~ 1 teaspoon lemon juice
Salt ~ Parsley sprigs ~ Lemon wedges
1 Tablespoon chopped green onion

Beat eggs and milk in a shallow dish. Mix flour, salt, and pepper in another shallow dish or on a piece of wax paper. Dredge catfish fillets in flour mixture, then in egg mixture and again in flour. Set aside on a wax-paper lined baking sheet. Pour oil into a deep fryer or a large, deep skillet and heat to approximately 360°F. Place fillets, two at a time, in hot oil and fry for 2 to 3 minutes on each side, or until golden brown and fish flakes easily when tested with a fork. Place on paper towels to drain.

While catfish are frying prepare the sauce. Heat 1 Tablespoon of the melted butter in a large skillet over medium heat. Add shrimp and sauté until light pink on both sides; do not overcook. Stir in garlic, ham strips and vermouth. Mix in cream, half of the green onion, lemon juice, salt, and cayenne pepper and cook for 1 to 2 minutes to reduce the cream. Remove from the heat and whisk in remaining 2 Tablespoons of butter. Place a catfish fillet on each serving plate and top with three shrimp pieces. Arrange ham strips to fill in gaps between the shrimp. Spoon sauce onto catfish and sprinkle with remaining green onion. Garnish with lemon wedges and parsley sprigs. You're likely to find some variation of this recipe if you order catfish anywhere in Louisiana.

This next recipe is absolutely gorgeous. Whoever you serve will think that you worked all day to create this catfish masterpiece. It is actually quite simple. If avocado, water chestnuts, and/or oranges are unavailable substitute boiled eggs for avocado, substitute tomatoes for oranges, and garnish with cooked snap beans instead of water chestnuts. Then call it **Catfish Chef Salad.**

Potpourri Salad with Catfish

Salad:
2 pounds catfish fillets, fresh or frozen
1 large avocado, peeled and sliced into rings
3 oranges, peeled and sectioned
1 pound fresh spinach, washed and torn into pieces
½ cup canned water chestnuts, sliced
3 strips bacon, cooked, drained and crumbled
1 tablespoon orange juice ~ 1 teaspoon salt

Salad Dressing:
⅔ cup salad oil ~ ⅓ cup orange juice
2 teaspoons sugar ~ ¼ teaspoon salt
½ teaspoon hot pepper sauce
¼ teaspoon dry mustard
½ teaspoon grated orange rind
1 Tablespoon white distilled vinegar

Garnish:
Water chestnuts ~ Bacon

Combine all salad dressing ingredients and mix thoroughly. Chill. Sprinkle fish with salt. Place fish in a well greased steamer pan and cook over boiling water for 10 to 12 minutes or until fish flakes with a fork. Remove fish, cool, and break into small pieces. Sprinkle avocado with orange juice. Combine fish, avocado, spinach and orange sections in a large salad bowl. Toss with salad dressing. Sprinkle with water chestnuts and bacon.

Delta Catfish Bisque

½ cup butter ~ 3 green onions, chopped
2 celery stalks, finely chopped ~ 2 catfish fillets
½ cup all-purpose flour ~ 4 cups milk
1 cup heavy cream ~ 1 teaspoon Tabasco sauce
1 Tablespoon chopped parsley ~ 1 bay leaf
1 Tablespoon chopped chives ~ 1 teaspoon salt

Melt 1 Tablespoon of the butter in a large saucepan over low heat. Add green onions, celery, and catfish fillets cut into 1-inch pieces. Sauté for 3 minutes; do not brown. Remove catfish and vegetables from the pan. Melt the remaining butter in the pan. Add the flour and stir for 2 to 3 minutes. Gradually stir in the milk and cream. Stir well after each addition. Cook, stirring constantly, until thickened. Add the catfish and vegetables. Stir in the Tabasco sauce, parsley, bay leaf, chives and salt. Simmer for 15 minutes and serve.

Smoky Catfish

4 catfish fillets ~ 1 teaspoon lemon juice
2 teaspoons liquid hickory smoke ~ 3 Tablespoons soy sauce
½ teaspoon garlic powder

Combine all ingredients except fillets in a small bowl and mix thoroughly. Coat broiling pan with a shortening spray. Place catfish in pan and coat both sides with mixture. Broil 3 to 4 inches from heat source for 4 to 6 minutes or until fish flakes when forked.

Beverages

In the South you can expect most beverages to be very sweet. Until I was married and on a trip outside of Mississippi I didn't know that people actually drank coffee or tea *without* lots of sugar. Fish Camp beverages are unique if only because they are always made fresh, using homemade recipes. I include a couple of my favorite Fish Camp beverage recipes below.

Sassafras Tea

Sassafras roots
(available at feed stores and fruit stands throughout the South)
1 cup sugar ~ Lemon ~ 1 gallon water

Wash sassafras roots and cut into pieces about 1 to 2-inches long.
Place in a deep boiling pot and cover with cold water. Bring to a
boil. Let boil for about 15 minutes. Strain roots and discard. Add
1 cup of sugar per gallon of tea. Squeeze lemon into tea and mix
well. Serve hot, over ice, or refrigerate.

In many Southern locales blueberries, huckleberries, and
blackberries are in plentiful supply. It is common to find these
berries made into a tea on Fish Camp menus.

Coffee

Lemonade, iced tea, and soft drinks are served in Fish
Camps these days, but coffee is the mainstay from the old days. As
I said in Chapter 1, coffee is made strong in the South. The basic
recipe most Southerners start with is 6 Tablespoons of ground coffee
per quart of water. It is certainly not unusual to find coffee made
much stronger. There are a number of more elaborate drinks,
uniquely Southern, that use strong coffee as a base. If you develop
a taste for strong coffee you'll go crazy over **Coffee Punch**.

Rich Coffee Punch

1 quart strong coffee ~ ½ gallon chocolate milk
3 teaspoons almond flavoring ~ 1 large container whipped
½ gallon vanilla ice cream topping

Make strong coffee and let it cool. Mash ½ gallon vanilla ice cream and mix together with all other ingredients. Serve cold. This recipe will serve about 50 people (1 serving).

Coffee Punch

1 gallon strong coffee ~ 3 quarts milk
1 gallon vanilla ice cream

Brew coffee and let it cool. Add milk and ice cream to coffee. Serve cold. This recipe will serve about 50 people (1 serving).

Get creative with coffee punches. Try any flavor or variety of ice cream that suits you, add lots of whipped topping to make it extra rich! Then create an authentic Southern Cider. Ciders come in a wide variety of flavors and potencies. The following is a typical, quick-to-prepare blend that uses a store-bought cider as a base that is dressed-up.

Southern Cider

1 orange, sliced (or ½ cup orange juice)
2 quarts apple cider (homemade if possible; store bought is OK)
1 teaspoon whole all spice ~ Whole cloves
2 cinnamon sticks ~ 2 cups water

Combine all ingredients in a 3 quart pot and bring to a boil. Reduce heat and simmer for 15 minutes. Serve fresh and hot or chill, and serve over ice. Try adding lemon and sugar for flavor or boiling with apples instead of oranges.

Chapter 5
Southern Nuts

When Southerners talk about **Southern Nuts** they may not be talking about the various hickory nuts that flourish, naturally, in the South. More often, they may be referring to one of the eccentric relatives in their particular clan. In most of the country people hide their crazy relatives. Not in the South. In the South they're made a part of everyday family life, carried around with us to every function and totally integrated into the Southern day.

When I was young I had an uncle that lived at the top of the hill up from our farm. He had been a college professor, until he snapped one day and became my childhood's nuttiest relative and perhaps the uncle I remember most fondly. The story goes that they found Ben running through the woods, naked. Today Ben might've been hauled off to a psychiatrist or nursing home. Then, he became a kind of babysitter for the smaller kids. We'd sit on his porch and listen to him give his "lessons." He wasn't necessarily talking to us, maybe to the trees or the sky or some long gone friends. Lessons continued until his death at the ripe old age of 96.

The other **Southern Nut**, the one that this cookbook would be incomplete without, is the pecan. In the 1940s and 1950s we would pick up pecans on halves. That meant that we could keep half of the nuts we collected for ourselves. The halve was our payment. We never ate them back then. The pecan was (and still is) one of the most valuable natural Southern commodities. Instead we'd work like a dickens trying to break open the very tough Hickory nuts that fell from the natural orchards around our farm. The Hickory is perhaps the toughest **Southern Nut** to crack and arguably provides the least amount of meat. Regardless, we made many of the recipes in this chapter with wild Hickory nuts rather than with valuable pecans. The history of American pecans is an interesting one. A summary of the story follows.

Pecans

There are 17 varieties of hickory trees, 13 that are native to the United States. The extremely hard hickory wood is widely used to smoke American hams. All varieties of the hickory tree bear nuts, the most popular being the pecan in part due to its thin shell. The pecan has a fat content of over 70% (see below), more than any other nut. Pecan trees prefer temperate climates which explains in part why they are found throughout the South from Virginia to Texas to Northern Florida. Native pecans evolved to their present state over a period of many centuries. There are many "improved" varieties introduced earlier this century that are still in their first few generations of evolution. Texas leads the nation in the production of native pecans with an estimated 600,000 acres and 30,000,000 individual trees. Pecans have potentially long life spans of over 150 years and grow to heights and canopy diameters of 150 feet or more. Huge pecan trees in the South are an awesome sight. They represent one of the South's natural treasures. Most Southerners know the big secret about pecans is that each pecan tree produces a nut that is its own unique variety. Many of us know a favorite tree that produces nuts perfectly suited to our individual pallette. There are literally tens of millions of unique pecan variations.

While native pecan trees are an evolutionary marvel, producing excellent flavored nuts, they pose problems for those who wish to produce commercial pecan crops. The pecan's limitations as an orchard tree (low average yields per acre, alternate and irregular bearing, unmanageable tree size, pests' competition for nuts, long juvenile stage, particular soil and water condition demands) are precisely the factors that have enabled it to compete effectively in its natural river bottom and lowland habitats.

For centuries, only American Indians knew the delicious taste of pecans. Since the 1500s, when European exploration and settlement of the South began, the popularity and demand for pecans has spread and grown. True commercial efforts at production date to the late 1800s. In the early 1900s the U.S. Department of Agriculture began pecan-breeding programs aimed at producing improved varieties of pecans that would in turn be more commercially viable. Much success has been achieved in cultivating large nuts with attractive meats and consistent size.

So how do you know a good pecan from a bad one? Two simple rules should be followed: Buy pecans in shell and don't buy any cracked nuts or ones that rattle when you shake them. For the really discerning cook there are some other things you might like to know. Pecans are generally rated by size and grades that include (from best to worst) Fancy, Choice, Standard, Damaged, and Inedible. Always look for Fancy or Choice pecans. Standards and Damaged pecans may be closer to the "Inedible" category than you might care for. Often when buying chopped pecan pieces you are really getting Damaged pecans that have been chopped. Don't be surprised when you bite into a hard shell. True Southern cooks take the extra time to shell and chop their own nuts! There are a few tips that will help you when buying in-shell pecans. First, examine the kernels and ask to taste a sample. Buy direct from the grower via the Internet or while traveling in the South. As in most business situations, the more middle men you can eliminate, the better your price will be. Third, when estimating your pecan needs, consider that about 2½ pounds of pecans will be needed to yield 1 pound (about 4 cups) of shelled pecans. Finally, be sure to plan for your pecan storage needs before you purchase the nuts. Because of their extremely high unsaturated oil content, pecans deteriorate rapidly at room temperature, especially after they are cracked. Pecans (in or out of the shell) will keep best in the freezer; Frozen pecans are good for about 2 years.

Pecans are a good source of potassium, thiamine, zinc, copper, magnesium, phosphorous, niacin, folic acid, iron, and vitamin B6. They also provide excellent fiber. Of their 70% fat content approximately 87% is unsaturated fatty acids (62% monosaturated and 25% polyunsaturated); definitely not for dieters.

The following nutty recipes are arrange by the part of the meal they occupy. Some are merely appetizers while others are part of a main course or dessert. All are delicious when homemade and served fresh!

Appetizers

Cinnamon Pecan Muffins

2 cups flour ~ ⅔ cup sugar ~ 1 Tablespoon sugar
½ teaspoon salt ~ 1 teaspoon cinnamon
½ teaspoon ground allspice ~ ¼ cup ground cloves
1 egg, slightly beaten ~ 1 cup milk
½ cup pecans, finely chopped
1 cup fresh or frozen cranberries, coarsely chopped

Preheat oven to 425°F. Butter a 12-cup muffin tin. Combine flour, sugar baking powder, salt and spices in mixing bowl; stir until well blended. Make a well in the center. In another bowl, blend thoroughly egg, milk and butter; pour mixture into well of dry mixture. Stir just until ingredients are moistened. Carefully fold in cranberries and pecans. Spoon batter into muffin cups about half full. Bake 20 to 25 minutes until lightly browned.

Pecan Corn Fritters

2 eggs ~ 1 cup flour ~ powdered sugar
2 teaspoons baking powder ~ 2 cups creamed corn
¼ cup sugar ~ ½ cup pecans, finely chopped

Mix all ingredients except powdered sugar together and drop by spoonsful into hot oil. Cook until brown, about 5 minutes. Turn over to brown other side. Remove and set of paper towels. Sprinkle with powdered sugar.
Makes about 30 fritters.

Pecan Ham Rolls

12 thin slices boiled ham
1 cup cream cheese
1 cup pecans, finely chopped
2 Tablespoons mayonnaise
1 clove garlic, chopped and mashed

Combine cream cheese, pecans, garlic, and mayonnaise; spread on ham. Roll and secure with fancy toothpicks. Served chilled.

Pecan Lemon Bread

¾ cup butter, softened ~ 1½ cups sugar ~ 3 eggs
2¼ cups flour ~ ¼ teaspoon salt ~ ¼ teaspoon soda
¼ cup buttermilk ~ 1 lemon rind, grated
¾ cups pecans, chopped ~ Juice of 2 lemons
¾ cup sifted powdered sugar

Combine butter and sugar, creaming until light and fluffy. Add eggs, beating well. Combine dry ingredients, adding buttermilk and dry ingredients alternately to creamed mixture, beginning and ending with buttermilk. Stir just until to moisten all ingredients. Stir in lemon rind and pecans. Spoon batter into a greased and floured 9 x 5 x 3-inch loaf pan. Bake at 325°F. for 1 hour and 15 minutes or until bread tests done. Cool 15 minutes; remove from pan. Combine lemon juice and powdered sugar; stir well. Punch holes in top of warm bread with wooden pick; pour on lemon glaze. Cool on wire rack. Cut into bite sized cubes and serve chilled.

Pecan Raisin Bread

1 cup sugar ~ 2 eggs, beaten
¼ teaspoon salt ~ 1 cup buttermilk
1 teaspoon soda ~ 2 cups flour
1 cup pecans, chopped
1½ cups raisins
2 teaspoon butter or margarine, melted

Combine sugar, eggs and salt. Combine buttermilk and soda; stir into sugar mixture. Add flour and beat until smooth. Add pecans, raisins and butter; mix well. Pour batter into a greases 9 x 5 x 3-inch loaf pan. Bake at 325°F. for 1 hour and 15 minutes or until done. Cool on a wire rack.

Pecan Strips

1½ cups pecans, chopped ~ 1⅓ cups flour
1½ sticks butter, softened
3 Tablespoons sugar
¼ teaspoon salt
1½ teaspoon vanilla extract
¾ cup powdered sugar
¼ cup unsweetened cocoa

Combine all ingredients except powered sugar and cocoa in a large bowl. Mix until thoroughly blended. Refrigerate 30 minutes. Mix cocoa and ¼ cup powered sugar. Preheat oven to 350°F. Sprinkle pastry cloth or board lightly with flour; roll out dough to ¼-inch thick. Cut into 3 x ½-inch strips. Place one-inch apart on ungreased cookie sheets. Bake 8 to 10 minutes, or until strips are set but not brown. Let stand 1 minute before removing to wire rack. Cool slightly. Roll half of the strips in powdered sugar and half in the cocoa mixture while still warm; cool completely. Serve cool. This recipe yields about 5 dozen.

Sweet and Celery Pecans

2 Tablespoons butter
1 cup peanuts
1 cup pecan halves
1 teaspoon celery salt
1 cup raisins
Stick butter

Melt butter in microwaveable dish. Add nuts and celery salt, stirring until nuts are covered with butter. Cook in Microwave for 6 minutes, stirring every two minutes. Add raisins. Serve warm.

Entrees

Southerners have found ways to dress up just about any entree imaginable, with pecans. From fried chicken to pork chops, there are recipes that add flavor and zest to a meal generally by adding a small amount of finely chopped pecans to the mix. The following represent some of the South's favorite made-with-pecan meals.

Pecan Cheese and Broccoli Casserole

1 pound fresh broccoli
1 can cream of chicken soup
½ cup milk
½ cup cheddar cheese, grated
1 cup pecans, chopped
½ cup bread crumbs

Cook broccoli in salted water until tender. Drain and place in a greased 1-quart casserole. Add cheese and pecans. Mix soup and milk and pour over broccoli. Top with bread crumbs and bake at 350° F. for 30 minutes.

Pecan Fried Chicken

1 frying chicken, cut up ~ 1 cup flour
1 ½ cups pecans, finely chopped ~ 1 cup cornmeal
2 teaspoons salt ~ 2 teaspoons black pepper
2 teaspoon cayenne pepper ~ 4 eggs
1 stick butter, melted ~ cooking oil

Heat cooking oil (about ½-inch of oil) in a deep frying skillet. Combine all dry ingredients in a bowl and mix well. In another bowl, mix eggs and butter. Dip chicken pieces into the egg mixture, and roll in dry mixture to coat thoroughly. Place chicken pieces in the heated skillet. Fry about 10 minutes on each side. Drain on paper towels before serving.

Pecan Lamb Chops

6 lamb chops, cut 1½-inches thick
1 cup dry cooking wine ~ ½ cup orange juice
1 Tablespoon chili powder ~ ½ cup pecans, chopped
2 Tablespoons olive oil ~ 1 medium onion, chopped
2 cloves garlic, minced ~ 1 teaspoon ground cumin
1 teaspoon salt ~ ¼ cup green chiles, cooked and diced

Place lamb chops in deep baking dish. Combine all other ingredients and mix well. Pour mixture over lamb chops and marinate overnight in refrigerator, turn chops after about 6 hours. Preheat oven to 450°F. Place chops in a roasting pan. Save marinade. Cook 15 minutes, then reduce heat to 350°F.; pour marinade over chops. Cook for 45 minutes or until meat is tender.

Pecan Pork Chop Casserole

6 pork chops, cut ½-inch thick
1 cup celery, chopped ~ 1 tablespoon cooking oil
2 cups rice ~ ¼ cup dried parsley flakes
4 cups water ~ 2 teaspoons dried basil, crushed
½ cup pecans, chopped ~ 2 tablespoons soy sauce
dash of paprika ~ 1 package onion-mushroom soup mix

Trim excess fat from chops and set aside. In a saucepan, sauté celery in oil until tender. Stir in rice, soup mix, parsley, basil and water. Bring to a boil. Remove from heat; stir in pecans. Turn mixture into a 9 x 13 x 2-inch baking dish. Place chops on top of rice mixture. Brush chops with soy sauce, sprinkle with paprika. Cover and bake at 350°F. for 25 minutes. Uncover and bake 10 additional minutes or until chops and rice are tender.

Pecan Stuffed Tomatoes

4 large tomatoes ~ ½ pound bacon
1 Tablespoon cooking oil ~ ½ cup onion, finely chopped
1 clove garlic, crushed ~ ¼ cup pecans, chopped
½ cup zucchini, diced ~ ½ bell pepper, diced
¼ teaspoon salt ~ 1 teaspoon basil leave ~ Dash pepper

Preheat oven to 350°F. Cut off the stem of each tomato; scoop out and reserve pulp, leaving ¼ thick shells. Turn tomatoes open end down to drain. Dice the reserved pulp. Heat bacon in a saucepan until cooked but not crisp. Remove bacon, saving the grease. Add oil, onion, and garlic to the bacon grease and sauté for 5 minutes. Add zucchini, bell pepper, salt, basil, Dash of pepper, and reserved diced tomato. Cook and stir over medium heat until vegetables are tender. Add pecans and bacon; stir gently to mix. Drain off liquid. Spoon mixture into tomato shells. Place in a shallow baking pan containing ½-inch water. Cover and bake 20 to 25 minutes or until tomatoes are tender.

Pecan Sweet Potatoes

2 pounds sweet potatoes ~ 1 stick butter or margarine
¼ cup brown sugar ~ 1 teaspoon honey
½ teaspoon nutmeg ~ ½ cup pineapple, crushed
½ cup pecans, chopped ~ 2 cups pecan halves

Cook unpeeled whole sweet potatoes in boiling water until tender then remove their skins. Mash until fluffy. Add all other ingredients. Pour into 1-quart buttered casserole. Bake at 400°F. for 20 minutes. Garnish with pecan halves.

Pecan Vegetables and Rice

2 tablespoons butter or margarine ~ 1 cup rice, uncooked
½ teaspoon salt ~ 2 cups chicken broth, hot
½ cup parsley, chopped ~ ½ cup green onions, chopped
½ cup celery, chopped ~ ½ cup pecans, chopped

Brown rice in butter and salt; pour into a casserole. Stir in broth. Cover and bake at 350°F. for 45 minutes. Add remaining ingredients and toss lightly. Bake 10 additional minutes.

The following section contains the real pecan favorites. Desserts. I've included everything from Pecan Fudge to Millionaires. There are several recipes for Pecan Pie and for Pecan Cookies, but you might want to try one of the more exotic desserts like Ambrosia or Tassies. They're all simple and simply delicious!

Desserts

Five Minute Pecan Fudge

2 tablespoons butter ~ 1⅔ cups sugar
½ teaspoon salt ~ ⅔ cup evaporated milk
2 cups miniature marshmallows
1½ cups semi-sweet chocolate pieces
¼ cup pecans, chopped

Combine butter, milk, sugar and salt in saucepan over medium heat. Bring to a boil. Cook 4 to 5 minutes, stirring constantly. Remove from heat. Stir in marshmallows, chocolate, vanilla and pecans. Stir vigorously for 1 minute, until marshmallows melt and blend. Pour into 8-inch buttered pan; cool. Cut into squares.

Golden Pecan Tassies

Pastry: 6 ounces softened cream cheese
1 cup butter ~ 2 cups flour

Filling: 2 eggs ~ 1½ cups brown sugar
2 teaspoons melted butter ~ ½ teaspoon vanilla
¼ teaspoon salt ~ 1 cup chopped pecans

Pastry: Blend cheese and butter. Gradually mix in flour to make a smooth dough. Shape dough into 1¼-inch balls. Put into 1¾-inch muffin wraps or 2¼-inch baking tins. Press firmly to completely cover bottom and sides, making a shell.

Filling: Beat eggs, sugar, butter, vanilla and salt until smooth. Sprinkle half of pecans over unbaked dough in cups. Spoon filling mixture into each cup, filling about ¾ full. Sprinkle each with rest of nuts. Bake at 350°F. for 15 minutes. Turn oven down to 250°F. and bake 10 minutes more. Makes about 3 dozen, depending on size of pans used.

Million Dollar Pecan Fudge

1 large can evaporated milk
4½ cups sugar
3 cups chocolate chips
2 jars marshmallow cream
1 cup pecans, chopped

Set marshmallow cream in hot water to soften. Stir and cook evaporated milk and sugar until it comes to a boil; remove from heat. Stir in chocolate chips, marshmallow cream and nuts. Grease pans and line with wax paper. Pour fudge in pans and let stand 8 hours. Turn out' take off wax paper and cut in squares.

Pecan Ambrosia

2 large oranges, peeled and cut into ¼-slices
¼ cup flaked coconut
¼ cup sour cream
1½ teaspoon brown sugar
¼ teaspoon grated orange rind
Pinch of salt
2 Tablespoons pecans, coarsely chopped

Place ⅓ of the orange slices in a medium size serving bowl. Top with about ⅓ of the coconut. Repeat the layers twice. Cover and refrigerate at least 1 hour. Combine sour cream and sugar; mix well. Stir in rind and salt for dressing; cover and refrigerate at least 1 hour. Top fruit with dressing and pecans before serving.

This **Pecan Ambrosia** recipe only makes 2 servings. You'll want to double or triple the basic recipe depending on your family size. For parties multiply ingredients by at least 10. Kids prefer whipped cream to sour cream and some just hate coconut. Try substitutions like maple or chocolate syrup that will please even the most particular taste!

Pecan Angel Pie

3 egg whites ~ 1 teaspoon vanilla extract
1 cup sugar ~ 1 cup graham cracker crumbs
1 cup pecans, chopped ~ 1 teaspoon baking powder
½ cup whipping cream or whipped topping

Beat egg whites and vanilla extract until soft peaks form; gradually add sugar, beating until stiff. Combine cracker crumbs, pecans and baking powder. Fold into egg white mixture. Spread into greased and floured 9-inch pie pan. Bake at 325°F. for 20 to 25 minutes. Cool completely and serve in wedges with whipped cream on top.

Pecan Cake

4 cups flour ~ 1 teaspoon salt
1 teaspoon baking powder
4 sticks butter, softened
2 cups sugar ~ 6 eggs, beaten
1 cup candied cherries
1 cup candied pineapple
4 cups pecans
2 teaspoons vanilla extract

Grease pan, then line bottom of pan with foil paper which has also been greased. Cream butter and sugar; add eggs and vanilla extract. Sift 3 cups of the flour, baking powder and salt; mix the remaining flour with the cherries, pineapple and nuts. Stir into batter. Cover top with foil paper. Bake at 350°F. for 2½ hours. Remove foil cover after an hour.

Pecan Chocolate Chip Oatmeal Cookies

3 cups flour ~ 2 teaspoons soda
2 teaspoon salt ~ 1½ cups powdered sugar
1½ cups brown sugar ~ 2 cups shortening
4 eggs ~ 2 teaspoons hot water
1 cup pecans, chopped ~ 1 cup chocolate chips
4 cups oatmeal ~ 2 teaspoons vanilla

Sift flour, soda and salt; set aside for later use. Cream sugars and shortening; beat in eggs; add hot water and vanilla. Add sifted ingredients; add nuts, chocolate chips and oatmeal. Mix well. Drop by spoonfuls on greased cookie sheet. Bake at 350°F. for 10 to 12 minutes. Makes about 16 dozen.

Mary Foley's Pecan Chocolate Delight

1 stick margarine ~ 1 cup flour
1 cup pecans, finely chopped ~ 1 cup cream cheese
1½ cups powdered sugar
1 carton (12 ounces) whipped topping
1 package (5 to 6 ounces) instant chocolate pudding
3 cups milk; 1 large can evaporated milk and whole milk

Mix margarine, flour and nuts; press into 9 x 12-inch dish. Bake at 350°F. for 20 minutes. Cool. Mix cream cheese and powdered sugar; add half of whipped topping. Pour onto cooled crust. Mix instant pudding with milk. Pour on top of cream cheese mixture. Top with remaining whipped topping. Sprinkle with pecans. Refrigerate overnight.

Pecan Chocolate Macaroons

4 egg whites ~ 1½ cups sugar
1 cup pecans, chopped ~ ¾ cup chocolate morsels

Beat egg whites until stiff, but not dry. Gradually add sugar, beating until mixture will hold its shape. Fold in pecans and chocolate morsels. Drop from teaspoon onto well greased cookie sheet. Bake at 350° F. for 20 minutes. Makes about 4 dozen coconut free macaroons.

Pecan Crunchy Topped Coffeecake

2 cups flour ~ 1 cup sugar
1 tablespoons baking powder ~ 1 teaspoon salt
1 cup milk ~ 1 stick butter or margarine, softened
1 egg ~ ½ cup pecans, chopped
¼ cup sugar ~ 1 teaspoon cinnamon

Sift flour, sugar, baking powder and salt into 3-quart bowl of electric mixer. Beat in milk, butter and egg at medium speed for 2 minutes, scraping sides of bowl often. Pour into greased and floured 9-inch square pan. Combine pecans, sugar and cinnamon in bowl. Mix thoroughly and sprinkle over batter. Bake at 350°F. for 35 minutes or until cake pulls away from sides of pan. Serve warm.

Pecan Date Cake

1 cup flour ~ 1 ½ cups pecans, chopped
1 cup dates, chopped ~ 1 cup sugar
3 eggs, beaten ~ ½ teaspoon baking powder

Mix half of flour with pecans and dates. Add remaining ingredients. Turn into greased cake pan. Bake at 275°F. for 45 minutes.

Pecan Graham Delight

1 cup pecans, chopped ~ 1 stick butter ~ ½ cup sugar
1 stick margarine ~ 1 box graham crackers

Preheat oven to 350°F. Separate crackers on cookie sheet. Spread pecans over crackers. Melt the butter, margarine, and sugar in pan over medium heat; let boil for 3 minutes. Stir occasionally. Pour over crackers and nuts. Bake for 10 minutes.

Pecan Pie

4 Tablespoons butter, softened ~ 1 cup sugar
1 teaspoon honey ~ 3 eggs, slightly beaten
1 cup light corn syrup ~ 1 teaspoon vanilla
Dash of salt ~ 1 cup pecans, chopped
9-inch pie shell, unbaked ~ Pecan halves

Cream butter and sugar then add remaining ingredients. Pour into pie shell. Top with pecan halves. Bake at 375°F. for 10 minutes, then reduce heat to 325°F. and bake for 30 to 35 minutes.

Pecan Pie, Fudge

1 deep dish pie shell ~ ½ cup butter
3 Tablespoons cocoa ~ ¾ cup hot water
2 cups sugar ~ ½ cup flour ~ Pinch salt
1 teaspoon vanilla extract ~ 1 5 ounce can evaporated milk
¾ cup chopped pecans

Preheat over and cookie sheet to 350°F. In a medium saucepan, melt butter. Add cocoa and stir until dissolved. Add hot water and stir again. With a wire whisk, stir in sugar, flour, salt, vanilla, and evaporated milk. Stir until batter is smooth. Mix in pecans and pour into pie crust. Bake on preheated cookie sheet for 50 minutes or until custard sets.

Pecan Pie, Golden

1 cup pecans, halves ~ 1 cup dark corn syrup
1 cup sugar ~ 3 eggs
2 tablespoons butter, melted ~ Dash of salt
1 teaspoon vanilla ~ 9-inch pie shell, unbaked

Mix corn syrup, sugar and butter with eggs. Add pecans, salt and vanilla; stir to blend. Pour into pie shell. Bake at 400°F. for 15 minutes, then reduce heat to 350°F. and bake an additional 25 to 30 minutes.

Pecan Pie, New Orleans Style

Like most Southerners my family has ties to the Big Easy. For us the trip to New Orleans once was an all day drive. Now most of Mississippi is now less than four hours from most of Louisiana. Needless to say, our cultures and foods are in some respects overlap. My Aunt Ethel insisted that New Orleans Pecan Pie was far superior to the countryfied version. You be the judge.

2 egg yolks ~ 1 cup sugar
8 ounces sour cream ~ ⅛ teaspoon salt
¼teaspoon lemon extract ~ 4 Tablespoons sifted flour
2 egg whites ~ 1 cup brown sugar
1 cup pecans

Mix and cook sugar, sour cream, salt, lemon, flour, and egg yolks in a double boiler until thick. Pour into a baked pie shell. Separately, beat egg whites until peaks hold. Add brown sugar to egg whites and blend well. Finally add nuts and blend. Cover pie with topping and bake at 325-350°F. until brown.

Pecan Pie, No-crust Chocolate

2 ounces sweet baking chocolate ~ ½ cup butter
1 teaspoon vanilla ~ 3 beaten eggs ~ 1 cup sugar
¼ teaspoon salt ~ 3 Tablespoons all-purpose flour
1 cup chopped pecans ~ whipped cream

In a saucepan melt chocolate and butter over low heat. Once melted, remove from heat and stir in vanilla. Then allow the mixture to cool. In a small mixing bowl combine eggs, sugar, flour, and salt. Beat with electric mixer until blended. Do not over mix. Fold in cooled chocolate mixture and nuts. Pour into a lightly greased and floured 9-inch pie plate. Bake in a 350°F. oven for 1 hour or until knife inserted just off-center comes out clean. Refrigerate the pie overnight. Before serving dollop with whipped cream and garnish with chopped pecans.

Pecan Torte

2 cups pecans, finely chopped ~ 5 eggs, separated
1 cup sugar ~ ⅔ cup butter, softened
½ cup toast crumbs, finely crushed ~ 1 teaspoon vanilla
Powered sugar ~ Pecan halves

In a large bowl beat egg whites at high speed until foamy. Gradually beat in ½ cup of the sugar until whites hold stiff, glossy peaks. In another bowl, beat together butter and remaining sugar until creamy. Beat in egg yolks and vanilla until fluffy. Mix in nuts and toast crumbs. Gently stir in about ⅓ of the beaten egg whites to lighten mixture. Gently fold in remaining whites until blended. Pour into a greased and floured 9-inch cake pan with removable bottom or spring-released sides. Bake at 350°F. for 45 to 55 minutes, until a toothpick inserted in center comes out clean and top spring back when gently touched. Let cool on a wire rack. Remove pan sides. Lightly sift powered sugar over top and garnish with pecan halves.

Quick Pecan Cookies

1 stick butter or margarine
1½ cups brown sugar
1 egg ~ 1½ cups flour
1 teaspoon vanilla extract
1 cup pecan halves

Cream butter with brown sugar and egg. Add flour, vanilla extract and pecans. Shape into little balls, place on buttered cookie sheet and flatten out to ⅛-inch thick rounds. Bake at 375°F. for 12 minutes until nicely browned. Makes 3 dozen.

Southern Pecan Cookies

1 cup butter ~ 1 cup confectioners sugar
2 teaspoons vanilla ~ 2¼ cups flour
2 cups chopped pecans ~ Confectioners sugar

Cream butter, sugar and vanilla. Gradually mix in flour and nuts. Roll dough into ¾-inch balls. Place 1½ inches apart on ungreased baking sheet. Bake at 300°F. for 30 minutes. While warm, roll in confectioners sugar. Cool and roll in sugar again. Makes about 6 dozen.

Sugared Pecans

1½ cups pecan halves
1 Tablespoon butter
½ cup sugar ~ ⅛ teaspoon cinnamon

Melt butter in a 9-inch pie plate. Stir in pecans halves, sugar and cinnamon and cook for 2 minutes in Microwave on High. Stir and cook for 2 additional minutes. Reduce power to 70% and cook an additional 1 to 1½ minutes.

White Pecan Fudge

2 cups sugar ~ ½ cup sour cream
⅓ cup light corn syrup ~ 2 tablespoons butter or margarine
¼ teaspoon salt ~ 2 teaspoon vanilla extract
¼ cup candied cherries, chopped
1 cup pecans, coarsely chopped

Combine sugar, sour cream, corn syrup, butter and salt in saucepan; bring to a boil over medium heat, stirring until sugar dissolves. Boil, without stirring, until a little mixture dropped in cold water forms a soft ball. Remove from heat and let stand 15 minutes. Add flavoring and beat until mixture starts to lose its gloss, 8 or 9 minutes. Quickly stir in cherries and pecans; then pour into greased 8 x 8-inch utility dish. Cool; cut into squares. Makes about 1 ½ pounds of fudge.

Chapter 6
Dinner-on-the-Ground

Dinner-on-the-Ground is a Southern custom that usually occurs on Sunday after church is over, after the smallest children have been put down for their naps, usually late in the afternoon when the heat has waned in summer or the ground had warmed in winter. It is perhaps the most relaxing, carefree time for storytelling, updates on families, and informal socializing. A lot of attention is paid to elderly family members. I've always enjoyed listening to the elderly recite the oral history of the South; storytelling is one of Dinner-on-the-Ground's favorite aspects for me. Of course I also love to finally relax and eat all I can possibly hold of other people's cooking!

In the old days everyone would bring their favorite dish, or bring what was seasonal; if it was butterbean time there would be dozens of butterbean dishes, if fruit was ripe there would be a table full of fresh pies. Whatever was in season along with some best-loved traditional foods would be brought together on a huge buffet table set up under the canopy of the church yard's biggest pecan tree. All of the church women would try to outdo one another with their fanciest cake and dessert recipes, or with the best fried chicken to be found in the county.

Today the tradition has changed in some larger communities. The community will gather in a large gymnasium or social hall. I think that those types of gatherings are missing the flavor and color of eating outdoors, watching the older kids play, fanning the flies away, and hoping that the thunderstorms stay at bay. If you travel deep enough into the Southern backwoods you're sure to find one of these get-togethers near country churches on sunny Sunday afternoons. Most churches would welcome you with open arms if you decided to stop and sample some of the local flavor.

There are literally hundreds of uniquely Southern recipes that I'd like to include in this chapter, but because of space limitations I instead offer a selection of what one would find at a typical Dinner-on-the-Ground. The different types of foods are separated by breads, meats, vegetables, and soups. Within the categories I've alphabetized the recipes so they appear much like you'd find them laid out under the trees; in no particular order. Don't look for fried recipes here though you would often find fried chicken and okra at a Southern Dinner-on-the-Ground. I've grouped all the fried favorites together in Chapter 8, Button Poppin' Fried Favorites.

Breads & Rolls

Broccoli Cornbread II

1 box cornbread mix ~ 4 eggs
2 cups grated cheese ~ 1 medium onion
1 box frozen chopped broccoli ~ 1 stick margarine

Mix all except margarine. Melt margarine in a 13 x 9-inch pan. Spoon batter into pan and bake at 400°F. for 30 minutes.

Buttermilk Cornbread

1 cup buttermilk
1 cup self-rising flour
½ cup flour ~ 1 egg, beaten
½ cup butter, melted

Melt butter in small skillet. Stir together the other ingredients. Add melted butter leaving small amount on bottom and sides of skillet. Pour mixture into heated skillet and bake at 350°F. for 25 to 30 minutes. Serve immediately. Freezes well after cooking.

Corned Beef & Tomato Biscuits

1½ cups all-purpose flour
3 teaspoon baking powder
½ teaspoon seasoned salt
mayonnaise ~ 1 cup milk
1½ cups chilled corned beef, cut in thin slices
prepared mustard ~ tomatoes, thinly sliced
Cheddar cheese, thinly sliced

Sift flour with baking powder and seasoned salt. Mix ½ cup mayonnaise with milk; carefully stir into sifted ingredients. On a lightly floured board, roll dough into an oblong about ½ -inch thick. Place on a baking sheet. Arrange corned beef to cover biscuit dough. Spread lightly with prepared mustard and mayonnaise. Cover with tomato slices; top with Cheddar cheese slices. Bake at 425°F. for 15 to 20 minutes, or until the biscuit base is golden brown. Cut in serving-size squares; serve hot.

Cracklin' Bread

2 cups self-rising cornmeal
1 cup dry milk ~ 1½ cup water ~ 1 egg
1 cup pork crackling, chopped in small pieces

Stir and pour into hot skillet. Bake at 350°F. for 30 minutes or until done.

Grandma's Homemade Rolls

1⅓ cups water, slightly warm
⅔ cup cooking oil
4½ Tablespoons sugar
1 egg, well beaten
1 package dry yeast ~ Dash of salt
4½ cups self-rising flour

Pour dry yeast into ⅓ cup water. Add 1 teaspoon of sugar. Stir to dissolve. Let mixture stand for 6 minutes. In a large bowl combine remaining sugar and water, oil, egg, and salt. Add yeast mixture. Add flour. Mix well until it becomes elastic-like in texture. Form into a ball and lay in a greased bowl. Let stand at room temperature for 2 hours or until doubled in size. Place on floured kneading board or wooden bowl; knead down and shape into balls. Place in large baking pan leaving space between each one to rise. Brush tops lightly with melted oil. Let stand for 2 hours. Bake a 425°F. for 20-25 minutes until tops are golden brown. Serve hot with butter, gravy or your favorite jelly. Yields 20.

Herbed Onion Bread

1½ cups finely chopped Spanish onions ~ 1 egg
1 Tablespoons butter or margarine ~ 1 cup milk
3 cups biscuit baking mix
1 teaspoon dried basil
1 teaspoon dried dill weed

Preheat oven to 350°F. In a large skillet saute the onion in the butter for 5 to 7 minutes until tender. Meanwhile, combine all remaining ingredients in a large bow. Add onions, mixing just until blended. Spoon into a greased 9 x 5-inch loaf pan. Bake for 55 to 60 minutes until golden. Cook before removing from pan.

Mexican Cornbread

1¾ cups self-rising flour ~ 1 cup cream
1 cup shredded cheese ~ 3 eggs
1 cup chopped onion
¾ cup cooking oil
½ cup milk ~ 1 teaspoon garlic salt
2 to 5 jalapeño peppers, chopped

Mix all ingredients and bake at 400°F. for 35 to 45 minutes.

Sour Cream Cornbread

1 cup self-rising cornmeal ~ 2 eggs
1 cup creamed corn
1 cup sour cream
½ cup salad oil

Combine all ingredients, mixing well. Pour into greased 9-inch pan
or iron skillet. Bake at 400°F. for 20 to 30 minutes.

Spoon Rolls

2 cups very warm water
1½ sticks margarine, melted
1 egg, beaten ~ 1 package active dry yeast
¼ cup sugar ~ 4 cups self-rising flour

Combine water and yeast. Cream melted margarine with sugar in
large bowl. Add dissolved yeast and flour. Stir until well blended.
Place in airtight bowl and refrigerate. When ready for rolls, drop by
teaspoonfuls into well-greased muffin tin and bake at 350°F. for 20
minutes or until brown. This mixture will keep for several days in
the refrigerator.

Sweet Potato Bread

3 cups sugar ~ 3½ cups flour
1 cup cooking oil ~ ⅔ cup orange juice
2 cups sweet potato ~ 4 eggs
1½ teaspoon salt ~ 1 teaspoon nutmeg
1 teaspoon cinnamon ~ 1 cup raisins
2 teaspoons soda ~ 1 cup chopped pecans

Mix all ingredients with electric mixer except for the pecans and raisins. Fold raisins and pecans into mixture. Bake at 350°F. for 1 hour. May use 2 loaf pans or four 1 pound coffee cans. Fill only ¾ full. Cool and remove from pans and wrap in plastic wrap.

Rich Blueberry Muffins

½ cup butter, softened
½ cup sugar
1 egg ~ ¾ cup milk
¼ teaspoon vanilla
1¾ cups flour
1½ teaspoon baking powder
½ teaspoon salt
1 cup blueberries (fresh or frozen), and tossed with flour

Cream butter and sugar until light and fluffy. Beat in egg, then milk and vanilla. Beat until nearly smooth. In small bowl, stir together flour, baking powder and salt. Add to milk mixture; stir just until dry ingredients are moistened. (Batter will be lumpy.) Fold blueberries into batter. Spoon into 12 greased muffin cups and cook in preheated oven at 400°F. for 25 minutes or until evenly golden brown.

Sausage-Sage Stuffed Biscuits

1 teaspoon Worcestershire sauce
1 pound hamburger
1 pound sage sausage
1 cup cream cheese
1 can biscuits

Brown meats and drain. Add cheese and sauce. Roll out biscuits and place a couple of spoons of the meat mixture in the center. Fold biscuits over and press around the edge with a fork. Bake until the biscuits brown. Serve warm.

Meats — Beef, Hamburger
Burgundy Burgers

2 pounds ground chuck (beef)
2 Tablespoons parsley, chopped
2 Tablespoons green onion, chopped
Salt and pepper to taste
1 cup dry red cooking wine
2 squares Roquefort or blue cheese

Mix ground chuck, parsley and green onion; season with salt and pepper. Shape in 8 patties, making a depression in the center of each. Place in a shallow pan and pour cooking wine over patties in the depressions. Chill 2 hours. Remove patties from marinade and broil over medium hot coals for 8 to 10 minutes for medium rare (can also be broiled in oven). Place a small square of cheese on each meat patty just before serving so it will melt slightly.

101

Crazy Meatloaf

1 10-ounce package frozen mixed vegetables
¼ cup butter or margarine ~ 1 medium onion, chopped
2 cups soft bread crumbs ~ ¼ cup chopped parsley
1¼ teaspoons salt ~ ¼ teaspoon thyme
¾ teaspoon hot sauce ~ 1 egg, slightly beaten
½ cup milk ~ ½ teaspoon basil
1½ pound ground steak ~ 1 cup grated Cheddar cheese

Cook the mixed vegetables in boiling, salted water for 5 minutes and drain. Melt butter in a skillet. Add the onion and cook until tender but not brown. Add bread crumbs, parsley, ¼ teaspoon salt, thyme and ¼ teaspoon hot sauce. Combine the egg, milk, remaining salt, basil and remaining hot sauce in a mixing bowl. Add 1 cup bread crumb mixture and mix well. Add the ground chuck and mix well. Press ¾ of the ground steak mixture over bottom and ¾ up the sides of a 9 x 5 x 3-inch loaf pan, leaving center hollow. Combine remaining bread crumb mixture with mixed vegetables and cheese and turn into beef mixture in loaf pan. Cover with remaining beef mixture. Bake in 350°F. oven for 1 hour. Let stand for 10 minutes before turning onto serving platter and serve with cheese sauce, if desired.

Meat Loaf, Family Style

1 pound lean ground beef ~ ½ pound lean ground pork
½ cup chopped onion ~ 1 egg, beaten
½ cup chopped green pepper ~ 1 Tablespoon chili powder
½ cup uncooked regular oats or cracker crumbs
½ teaspoon salt ~ ½ teaspoon pepper
tomato gravy

Combine all ingredients except the tomato gravy; shape into an 8-inch loaf and place in a 9 x 5 x 3-inch loaf pan. Pour tomato gravy over meat loaf and bake at 350°F. for 1 hour or until done.

Southern Beef Stew

2 pounds beef stew meat, cut in 1 inch cubes
¼ cup all-purpose flour ~ 1½ teaspoon salt
1 can cream of mushroom soup ~ ½ teaspoon pepper
1 teaspoon Worcestershire sauce ~ 1 can beef broth
1 teaspoon garlic salt ~ 1 teaspoon paprika
4 to 5 carrots, sliced
3 to 4 potatoes, diced
2 cup green peas, drained
2 teaspoons gravy,
browning sauce

Toss meat with flour, salt, and pepper. Place in a slow cooker; add the remaining ingredients and stir to mix well. Cover and cook on low for 10 to 12 hours or 4 to 6 hours on high. Stir before serving. Very good with hot corn bread.

Stuffed Bell Peppers II

10 bell peppers ~ 2 onions
2½ pounds lean ground beef ~ 2 cans canned whole tomatoes
3 to 4 fresh tomatoes ~ 5 cups cooked rice
salt and pepper ~ Dash of garlic salt and chili powder

Clean peppers, remove top and boil in salted water about 7 minutes. Chop pepper tops and onion into the hamburger meat and cook until gray; add tomatoes and cooked rice. Drain pepper and fill with meat mixture. Put extra in bottom of casserole and bake at 350° F. for about 30 minutes. Garnish with add salt, pepper, garlic salt and chili powder.

Chicken

Chicken Breast with Mushrooms

5 whole chicken breasts, cut in 10 pieces
5 cups flour ~ 2½ teaspoons salt
2½ teaspoon paprika ~ 2½ teaspoon nutmeg
2½ teaspoon pepper ~ 1 stick butter
2½ cups heavy cream ~ 1 cup cooking sherry
40 medium-sized mushrooms, sliced

Dust chicken breast with a mixture of the flour and spices. Melt butter in a chafing dish over direct heat; brown chicken on both sides (about 15 minutes). Remove chicken, stir in half of the cream and all of the sherry. Return chicken to chafing dish, cover and cook slowly for about 20 minutes or until the chicken is tender. Add remaining cream and mushrooms; cook 10 more minutes.

Chicken Loaf, Southern

1 cup soft bread crumbs ~ 2 egg, lightly beaten
2 cup milk ~ ½ teaspoon salt
½ teaspoon paprika ~ ½ cup peas
3 cups chicken, cooked and diced ¼-inch thick
½ cup pimento, chopped
1 can cream of mushroom soup for sauce

Blend bread crumbs, eggs, milk, salt and paprika in a bowl. Stir in chicken, peas and pimento. Turn into a well-greased loaf pan. Bake at 325°until firm, about 40 minutes. Serve with the mushroom sauce.

Chicken Salad, Hot!

4 cups cold chicken, cooked and cut up into chunks
2 Tablespoons lemon juice ~ toasted almonds, finely chopped
½ cup mayonnaise ~ 1 teaspoon salt
½ teaspoon monosodium glutamate, if available
1 cup grated cheese ~ 2 cups celery, chopped
4 eggs, hard-boiled and sliced ~ ½ cup cream of chicken soup
1 teaspoon onion, finely minced ~ 2 pimentos, finely cut
1½ cups potato chips, crushed

Combine all ingredients except cheese, potato chips, and almonds. Place in a large rectangular dish. Top with cheese, potato chips and almonds. Refrigerate overnight. Preheat oven to 400°F. Bake for 20 to 25 minutes.

Chicken-Vegetable-French Fry Casserole

2 fryer chickens, cup up ~ 1½ sticks butter, melted
½ cup flour ~ 1 can cream of celery soup
1½ cups frozen peas and carrots ~ 1 pound frozen french fries
Parmesan cheese

Cook, cool, and bone chicken. Reserve 2 cups of broth. Place chicken in a buttered 9 x 13-inch pan. Combine half of butter; flour, salt, soup and reserved broth for sauce. Cook until thick and smooth. Cook peas and carrots for 3 minutes. Drain. Mix peas and carrots with sauce and pour over chicken. Stir french fries in remaining butter until coated. Place on top of other ingredients. Sprinkle generously with Parmesan cheese. Bake at 450°F. for 20 to 25 minutes.

Southern Style Cream Chicken

1½ cups frozen creamed chicken, thawed
½ cup boiled ham, diced
1 Tablespoon butter or margarine
½ teaspoon prepared mustard
Cheddar cheese, several strips sliced
4 servings instant mashed potatoes

Heat creamed chicken slowly to simmering in a saucepan. Cook diced ham quickly until lightly browned in butter or margarine; add to creamed chicken along with mustard. Spoon chicken into prepared ring of Duchess potatoes (see recipe below). Lay strips of cheese across the chicken. Place under broiler until cheese is bubbling and potatoes are lightly browned.

Duchess Potatoes
4 servings instant mashed potatoes
2 eggs ~ 1 teaspoon butter or margarine
Salt to taste

Prepare instant potatoes according to directions on box. Season potatoes with salt and butter or margarine. Beat in 2 egg yolks. On a board or oven-proof tray, spoon potatoes in a ring and brush with slightly beaten egg white. Fill with Southern Style Creamed Chicken (see recipe above).

Ham
Baked Herb Stuffed Ham

4 Tablespoons butter or margarine
1 onion, finely chopped
10 mushrooms, finely chopped
1½ teaspoons prepared mustard
2 Tablespoons parsley, finely chopped
2 Tablespoons chives, finely chopped
½ teaspoons ground sage
½ cup herb bread crumbs
Salt and pepper to taste ~ Chicken stock
6 slices boiled or baked ham, ¼ to ½-inch thick

Heat 2 tablespoons butter in skillet; add onion and mushrooms; saute 5 minutes; remove to bowl. Add all other ingredients except butter and ham with enough chicken stock to moisten the mixture and hold it together. Spread the mixture on the ham slices; fold slices in half; arrange on shallow buttered baking dish. Melt the remaining butter and pour over ham slices. Cover. Bake at 275°F. for 20 minutes.

Boiled Southern Stuffed Ham

1 cured ham (10 to 12 pounds) ~ 2 pounds kale, chopped fine
3 medium heads cabbage, chopped fine
8 medium onions, chopped fine ~ 2 teaspoons salt
1 teaspoon red pepper ~ 1 teaspoon black pepper
3 teaspoons celery seed ~ 3 teaspoons mustard seed
1 teaspoon dry mustard

Mix kale, cabbage, onions and seasonings thoroughly. Using a sharp knife, cut 6 to 8 deep pockets into the top of the ham and fill each with as much stuffing as possible. Place any remaining stuffing on the top and around the ham. Put ham and dressing in a cooking bag; secure bag tightly in order to keep dressing in place. Put bag on a rack in pot and cover with water. Boil 20 minutes for each pound of ham. When done, remove ham from pot and place on rack until it cools. Serve cold. Keep any leftovers well refrigerated.

Pork
Pork Chops, Breaded

6 pork chops ~ ¼ cup fine bread crumbs
1 teaspoon salt ~ 1 teaspoon pepper
1 egg, beaten ~ ⅛ cup milk ~ ⅛ cup boiling water

Mix bread crumbs, salt and pepper. Separately, beat egg and milk. Dip pork chops in milk and roll in crumbs. Put 3 Tablespoons fat in skillet; brown pork chops. Place pork chops in a baking pan or dish and add boiling water. Cover and bake at 400°F. for about 50 minutes.

Uncle Lewis' Pork Chops, Lemon Glazed

1 or 2 pork chops per person ~ salt and pepper
2 to 3 teaspoons prepared mustard
½ teaspoon grated lemon peel ~ 1 teaspoon lemon juice
½ cup brown sugar ~ lemon slices

Preheat the broiler. Score thin pork chops and broil 3 or 4 inches from heat until well browned; Season with salt and pepper, then broil other side. Blend prepared mustard, lemon peel , lemon juice and brown sugar. Spoon blended mixture over each chop; top with a thin lemon slice and return to broiler until mixture bubbles and browns slightly.

Pork Chops, Soupy

6 pork chops, ½-inch thick, fat trimmed
1 can tomato soup ~ 1 package dry onion soup mix
1 medium onion, sliced ~ 1 green pepper, sliced
1 cup mushrooms, sliced

Arrange chops in an oblong casserole. Mix remaining ingredients and pour over chops. Cover with wax paper. Microwave at 70% for 30 minutes.

There are a couple of meaty specialties that just don't quite fit in one of the other categories. The miscellaneous meat recipes follow.

Sausage and Macaroni Casserole

2 cups macaroni in cheese sauce
1½ cups frozen green beans, cooked and drained
1 teaspoon prepared mustard
1 can Vienna sausage, drained
1 Tablespoons grated Parmesan cheese

Spoon macaroni and cheese around the edge of a shallow 8-inch casserole. Mix beans with mustard and place in center of macaroni. Arrange sausages on macaroni; sprinkle with grated cheese. Bake, uncovered, at 350°F. for 15 minutes or until thoroughly heated.

Turkey Chili

1 pound ground turkey ~ ½ cup chopped bell pepper
¾ cup cooked kidney beans ~ ½ cup chopped onion
3 medium tomatoes, peeled and chopped
1 teaspoon chili powder ~ 1 clove garlic, minced
½ teaspoon dried oregano leaves ~ 1 cup water
⅛ teaspoon ground red pepper ~ ¾ cup no salt tomato paste
½ teaspoon ground cumin

In a large heavy pot, brown turkey and pour off any excess fat. Add onions, green pepper and garlic. Cook 2 minutes, stirring constantly; add beans, water, tomatoes, tomato paste, chili powder, oregano, cumin and red pepper. Mix together real well, cover and let simmer for 1½ hours.

Vegetables
Asparagus with Cashew Butter

2 cups fresh asparagus or 1½ cup frozen asparagus spears
1 cup butter ~ 2 teaspoons lemon juice ~ ½ teaspoon marjoram
1 cup salted cashews, broken in lengthwise halves

Cook asparagus in salted water about 12 minutes until tender (for frozen asparagus, cook as directed on package). Drain cooked spears and arrange on a serving dish. Melt the butter in a small pan; add lemon juice, marjoram and cashews. Simmer over low heat for 2 minutes. Pour over the cooked asparagus and serve.

Copper Pennies

4 cups sliced carrots, canned or fresh cooked until tender
1 small bell pepper, cut in strips ~ 1 medium onion, cut rings
1 can tomato soup ~ ¾ cup vinegar
1 cup sugar ~ 1 teaspoon mustard
1 Tablespoon Worcestershire sauce ~ ½ teaspoon salt
¼ teaspoon black pepper

In saucepan combine tomato soup, oil, vinegar, sugar and seasonings; bring to boil and pour over vegetables. Refrigerate overnight.

Corn Casserole

1 can whole corn with liquid ~ 1 can cream corn
1 cup sour cream ~ 1 cup mild cheddar cheese
1 onion, chopped ~ 1 bell pepper, chopped
1 box corn muffin mix ~ 1 stick margarine.

Melt margarine in casserole dish, mix other ingredients. Pour in dish. Bake at 375°F. for 30 minutes.

Creole Okra

1 medium onion, sliced ~ 1 small clove garlic, crushed
2 pounds okra, cut in ½ inch slices
1 teaspoon Worcestershire sauce
Salt and pepper to taste ~ 1 medium size bell pepper, diced
¼ cup bacon drippings ~ ¼ teaspoon sugar
4 medium tomatoes, peeled and chopped
Hot cooked rice

Sauté onion, bell pepper, and garlic in bacon drippings in a Dutch oven until onion is tender. Add in other ingredients except rice. Cover and cook over medium heat about 20 minutes. Remove from heat. Serve over rice.

Fluffy Cheese Rice

1 cup uncooked rice ~ 2½ cups chicken broth
1 Tablespoon butter ~ dash powdered saffron
½ cup hot water ~ 1 cup shredded Swiss cheese

Combine rice and chicken broth in a pan; add butter and bring to a boil. Cover, turn heat to lowest setting and cook for 20 minutes or until rice has absorbed the liquid. Combine saffron with hot water and stir to dissolve completely. Add to the rice after it has cooked 10 minutes. When the rice is cooked, fold in Swiss cheese. Do not stir or the cheese will get stringy. Serve hot.

Nut-Brown Vegetable Pie

1 cup cooked lima beans, drained
2 cups cooked whole kernel corn, drained
1 cup onions, finely chopped ~ 2 cups cooked tomatoes
¼ teaspoon pepper ~ 2 teaspoon salt
2 cups sifted flour ~ 3 teaspoons baking power
1 teaspoon salt ~ 5 Tablespoons shortening
½ cup peanut butter ~ ¾ cup milk

Preheat oven to 450°F. Combine vegetables and seasonings and place in a greased casserole. Put casserole in oven and bake about 25 minutes, or until vegetables are boiling. Meanwhile make biscuit topping as follows: Sift flour with baking power and salt. Cut in shortening until mixture is like meal. Then cut peanut butter in fine. Add milk, mixing until a soft dough is formed. Drop by spoonfuls on boiling hot vegetables in casserole. Bake at 450°F. for about 25 minutes.

Quick Potatoes

2 cups frozen browned potato slices
3 Tablespoons butter
3 Tablespoons minced parsley

Spread potato slices in a single layer on a rimmed baking sheet. Heat at 425°F. for 20 to 25 minutes. Melt butter in a saucepan. Stir in parsley. Place potatoes in a small, deep serving bowl and pour parsley butter over them. Makes 2 or 3 servings.

Stuffed Baked Potatoes

Potatoes, baked ~ Milk
Butter ~ Seasonings
Chopped onion ~ Beaten egg white
Grated cheese

Cut a slice from top of baked potato or half a large baked potato lengthwise. Scoop out inside; mash and add milk, butter, and seasonings. Beat until fluffy; pile tightly into shells and return to oven to brown slightly. If desired, add finely chopped onion or stiff beaten egg white or sprinkle with grated cheese before returning to oven.

Sweet Onion Stir-fry

2 large sweet onions ~ 2 to 3 medium-sized zucchini
2 to 3 tablespoons peanut oil ~ 1 Tablespoon sesame seed
Salt and pepper to taste ~ garlic powder (optional)

Peel the onions and slice in half lengthwise; then slice into strips along the grain of the onions, forming strips about ½ inch wide. Wash zucchini and trim away ends. Cut each zucchini in half lengthwise, then cut crosswise into ½ inch slices. In a large skillet or wok, heat peanut oil; saute onions, zucchini, and sesame seeds over high heat, stirring frequently. Cook vegetables until just tender; remove from heat. Add salt, pepper, and garlic powder.

Squash Soufflé

1 pound squash ~ 1 onion, grated
Salt ~ 10 saltine crackers ~ 1 cup grated cheddar cheese
¼ cup margarine ~ ½ cup milk ~ 2 eggs

Stew squash until tender. Mix all the remaining ingredients with the cooked squash. Pour into a baking dish and bake at 300°F. for 30 minutes.

Yummy Yams

6 medium sweet potatoes ~ ¼ cup brown sugar
½ stick margarine ~ ½ teaspoon cinnamon
¼ cup orange juice ~ ½ cup crushed pineapple
10 ounces marshmallows

Cook sweet potatoes until tender; peel and mash. Combine other ingredients, top with marshmallows and bake at 375°F. for 20 minutes.

Soups, Southern Style

Warm soups add a special touch to wintertime Dinner-on-the-Ground gatherings. These are four of the South's easiest, and best!

Southern Corn Soup

1 can cream style corn ~ 1¼ cups milk
½ cup green onions, chopped
dash of pepper ~ 1 teaspoon honey
2 Tablespoons butter or margarine

Put corn, onions, and milk in a blender and whirl for ½ minute. Add pepper and honey and blend well. Strain into a sauce pan pushing as much of the soup mixture through the strainer as possible. Add butter and stir over medium heat. Garnish with paprika. Serve warm.

Cream of Cabbage Soup

2 to 3 cups cabbage, shredded
2 Tablespoon butter or margarine
1 medium onion, minced
1 garlic clove, crushed ~ 3 cups chicken stock
2 teaspoons flour ~ 1 egg yolk
½ cup evaporated milk ~ Cheddar cheese, grated
Pinch of pepper, salt, nutmeg, and thyme

Saute onion and garlic in butter until light brown. Stir in flour and add stock. Cook four minutes. Add cabbage and cook over low heat for 25 minutes. Pour into blender and whirl until smooth. Return to pan. Beat egg and evaporated milk with a fork. Stir a bit of hot soup into the egg mixture and then back into the soup. Reheat over low heat so it won't boil. Stir. Season to taste. Ladle into bowls and garnish with cheese.

Southern Style Pea Soup

1¼ cup frozen green peas
¼ cup ham or bacon, diced
3 Tablespoons butter ~ 1 medium onion
2 medium carrots ~ ½ teaspoon salt
¼ teaspoon lemon pepper ~ ¼ teaspoon curry
1 cup chicken stock ~ 1 cup cream
Parmesan cheese

Brown ham in butter; add onion and carrots, allowing them to brown. Pour in stock and simmer for an hour. Add peas, cook ten minutes and pour all into the blender. Whirl until smooth. Strain back into the pan, reheat to simmer. Add seasonings. Garnish with Parmesan cheese.

Cream of Spinach Soup

1 package frozen chopped spinach, thawed
3 Tablespoons butter or margarine
2 medium carrots, shredded
1 medium onion, minced
1 clove garlic, crushed ~ ½ teaspoon salt
2 cups stock ~ pinch of nutmeg ~ pinch of lemon pepper
1 teaspoon honey ~ 1 cup cream ~ egg, hard-boiled

Saute carrots, onion, and garlic in butter. Add spinach. Stir and cook 5 minutes, add stock and seasonings. Cook another 30 minutes. Add cream and reheat but do not boil. Add seasonings, blending well. Garnish with sliced hard-boiled egg.

Salads & Sauces
Blueberry Salad

2 3-ounce packages blackberry gelatin or black cherry gelatin
2 Tablespoons sugar
2 cups boiling water
4 cups blueberries, canned ~ 2 cups creamed cheese
2 cups crushed pineapple, canned ~ ½ cup sugar
1 cup sour cream ~ 1 small jar cherries
½ cup chopped pecans

Dissolve gelatin and 2 teaspoons sugar of sugar in hot water. Add fruit. Add 1 more cup liquid (juice drained from fruit). Pour into a flat dish and chill until firm. Combine cream cheese, sugar, and sour cream in blender. Spread over chilled gelatin. Add chopped pecans and drained cherries. Chill.

Myrrh-Lorraine's Broccoli Salad

1 bunch fresh broccoli, chopped into bite-sized pieces
1 cup grated cheese ~ 1 red onion
1 cup bacon bits ~ ¼ cup sugar
1 cup salad dressing ~ ¼ cup red wine vinegar

Make layers of broccoli, cheese, and onions. Top with bacon bits.
Mix salad dressing, vinegar, and sugar; pour over salad.

Buttermilk Salad

1 20-ounce can crushed pineapple
1 large package Jell-O (any flavor)
2 cups buttermilk ~ 3 cups Whipped topping

Pour pineapple with juice in boiler along with Jell-O. Mix well;
bring to a boil, stirring constantly. Remove from heat, pour into
serving dish and refrigerate until it starts to thicken. Then stir in
buttermilk and Whipped topping. Return to refrigerator until set.

Cherry Salad

1 medium size can crushed pineapple, drained
1 can condensed milk ~ 1 can cherry pie filling
2 cups Whipped topping ~ 1 cup chopped pecans

Mix all ingredients and chill.

Odessa's Potato Salad
Sour Cream Style

8 medium potatoes, sliced and boiled in peel
½ cup mayonnaise ~ 1 cup sour cream
½ teaspoon salt ~ 1½ teaspoons horseradish sauce
1 cup fresh parsley ~ 1 teaspoon celery seed (optional)
1 cup chopped green onions
dash of coarse black pepper

Combine sour cream, mayonnaise and horseradish; layer with other ingredients (do not toss). Cover and refrigerate overnight.

Spinach and Tomato Salad

10 bunches spinach ~ 100 cherry tomatoes
French dressing

Wash spinach well and drain; tear into small pieces. Halve tomatoes; mix with the spinach. Dress with French dressing just before serving. Serves about 20.

Chapter 7
Mississippi Mud and other Southern Desserts to Die For

Southern desserts are arguably the best in the world. Years of refinement, testing, and tasting by the best home spun cooks around have created some incredible confections. My absolute favorite is the Mississippi Mud Torte, a combination of pie and souffle. I'll get to that recipe soon enough, first I share homemade recipes for glaze, icing, and fudge.

Homemade Decorator Frosting

½ teaspoon salt ~ ½ cup water
2 teaspoons vanilla ~ ⅓ cup powdered coffee creamer
¾ cup shortening ~ 5 cups confectioners sugar (sift if lumpy)

Measure all ingredients into large bowl. Mix at medium speed for 3 minutes, then at high speed for 5 minutes. Add more sugar to thicken or more water to thin frosting, as required until it is at spreading consistency. Makes about 3¾ cups. Take wax paper to make tubes for cake decorating. Colors make frosting smoother, use extra stiff for adding color to cake. If frosting remains, it can be stored by covering tightly and storing in refrigerator.

Homemade Chocolate Fudge

2 cups sugar ~ ½ cup white Karo Syrup
½ cup milk ~ 2 Tablespoons cocoa
1 teaspoon vanilla ~ 1 stick butter
1 cup chopped nuts (or more as you like it)

Mix sugar and cocoa thoroughly then add syrup and milk. Mix over high heat until the mixture forms a soft ball when dropped into cold water. Then add vanilla and butter and mix completely again, before removing from pan. Pour the hot mixture into a mixing bowl and mix at high speed until it becomes thick and creamy. Add nuts and stir until mixture is thick enough to be cropped on wax paper or put in buttered dish and cut into squares, or poured atop a fresh, hot Mississippi Mud Cake.

Now that we covered the standard way to make fudge or decorator's frosting, lets learn how to make it in a hurry. This is my own special "quicky" Fudge or Frosting recipe, perfected over the years while rasing my three sugar-loving boys.

Lola's Quicky Fudge or Icing

1 box powdered sugar ~ 1 stick butter or margarine
3 Tablespoons cocoa (more or less)
¼ cup milk or half and half (start with less, then add if needed)
1 teaspoon vanilla (or more, to taste)

Mix ingredients together in pot on stove top. Cook until boiling. After mixture reaches boil, remove from heat and let cool for a few minutes. Beat until mixture is of spreading consistency. For Fudge pour onto greased plate. For Icing, spread warm onto cake or brownies.

What Southern cookbook would be complete without a recipe for Mississippi Mud Cake? Not this one! We've seen dozens of variations on this favorite and yet only have one enduring recipe that pleases time and time again.

Mississippi Mud Cake

4 eggs ~ 2 cups sugar ~ 1 Tablespoon cocoa
2 sticks butter, melted ~ 1½ cup self-rising flour
1 teaspoon vanilla ~ 1 cup chopped nuts
17-ounce jar of marshmallow cream

Gather eggs, sugar, cocoa, and melted butter. Beat together until smooth. Gradually add flour, mixing into batter. Once the batter is mixed well, add vanilla and nuts. Pour into 9 x 13-inch baking dish and bake 30-40 minutes at 350°F. When done remove from oven. Cake is done when toothpick inserted into the middle of the cake is clean when removed, or lightly palm on top of cake, if it is firm, it is likely done. Spread 1 7 ounce jar of marshmallow cream over the top of cake and put back into the over for 10-15 minutes. Remove from oven again and ice cake with a mixture of the following, without removing it from the pan.

1 box 10x powdered sugar ~ 2 Tablespoons cocoa
enough evaporated milk to spread

When cool, cut into blocks to serve.

A variation that works equally well, and is a little less trouble, is to top with a layer of chocolate fudge, prepared as you like it (using above recipe).

Considering that we were busy in the fields and at school and knew little about the outside world it is surprising how many of the old recipes allude to sex, money, or other worldly pleasures that were largely foreign to rural Mississippians prior to the current generation. I remember blushing when my mama would talk about making her **Better Than Sex Cake**. I also remember dreaming of castles and mansions when she pull out the dog-eared recipe notes that included **Millionaires** and **Divinity**. Somehow she did it all without a refrigerator, electric blender, or a weather forecast. Today's cookbooks seem to require all of the above for some of our favorite old recipes. Below are the old recipes, updated for those who insist on using electricity.

Better Than Sex Cake

1 box yellow cake mix ~ ¾ cup coconut
1 20-ounce can crushed pineapple and juice ~ ¾ cup sugar
2 boxes (3½ ounce each) vanilla pudding
1 cup heavy or whipping cream
¼ cup confectionery (10x) sugar ~ 1 teaspoon vanilla

Bake cake according to the box directions in a rectangular pan. Meanwhile cook the crushed pineapple, its juice, and the sugar until thick (about 20 minutes). Once the cake is done and cool, repeatedly pierce it with a fork then pour the pineapple mixture over the cake. Blend pudding and milk and spread it atop the pineapple mixture. Blend cream, powdered sugar, and vanilla until it peaks. Spread it atop the pudding mixture. Sprinkle coconut over the top (or nuts, or decorative sprinkles). Refrigerate for 24 hours and serve.

Millionaires

1 bag light caramels ~ 2 cups pecans
1 bag milk chocolate chips ~ ½ paraffin wax bar
2 Tablespoons milk

Melt caramels, add milk, and mix well. Add pecans to the mixture.
Drop mixture onto wax paper by the spoonful. Take the remaining
ingredients (chocolate chips and paraffin) and melt in a pan placed
in a second pan of hot water. The caramel mixture should be firm
by the time chip-paraffin mixture is fully melted. Dip caramel blobs
into melted chocolate wax. Let dry on wax paper.

Lola's Low Calorie
Black Forest Cheesecake

¾ cup bear-shaped chocolate graham cracker cookies, crushed
Butter-flavored cooking spray ~ ¼ cup unsweetened cocoa
2 12-ounce packages fat-free cream cheese product, softened
¾ cup egg substitute ~ 1½ teaspoons vanilla extract
1 cup semisweet chocolate morsels, melted (6 ounces)
18-ounce carton nonfat sour cream alternative
1 21-ounce can reduced-calorie cherry pie filling
¾ cup reduced-calorie frozen whipped topping, thawed.

Spread cookie crumbs on bottom of 9-inch spring from pan coated
with cooking spray and set aside. Beat cream cheese at high speed
with a mixer until fluffy; gradually add sugar, beating well. Slowly
add egg substitute, mixing well. Add melted chocolate, cocoa, and
vanilla, mixing until blended. Stir in sour cream. Pour into
prepared pan. Bake at 300°F. for 1 hour and 40 minutes. Remove
from oven. Run a knife around edge of pan to release sides. Let
cool completely on a wire rack then cover and chill at least 8 hours.
Remove sides of pan and spread cake with cherry pie filling. Dollop
each serving with 1 tablespoon whipped topping. For a creamier-
textured cheesecake, bake at 300°F. for 1 hour and 20 minutes.

Great Grandmother Rosa's
Pound Cakes

These old family recipes have been passed down since before the Civil War. My great grandmother Rosalind (Rosa) Allen Leggett lived in McComb, Mississippi. Her pound cakes fed Union and Confederate soldier alike. The story goes that she figured the Yankees would be slowed by her heavy desserts, and what choice did she have anyway? She recounts some of her experiences in salvaged letters dating back to the mid-19th century. Imagine what she would think if she knew that her recipes had been imitated across the country. You can go into practically any large supermarket (that contains a "fresh" bakery) and find some variation of the Mt. Olive Pound Cake. Those imitations are prepared in huge bakeries, frozen, and shipped across the country. Yours will be authentic, hot, and truly fresh. In Mississippi, we take pound cake (regardless of the variety), slice it about 1 inch thick, and fry it lightly in butter. Add a scoop of homemade ice cream and you have a favorite Southern dessert.

Rosa's Butter Pound Cake

2 sticks butter ~ 1 box confectioners sugar
6 eggs ~ 2½ cups cake flour,
or regular four sifted 5 times after measuring
1 teaspoon coconut flavoring
1 teaspoon almond flavoring
1 teaspoon vanilla flavoring
½ cup finely chopped walnuts or pecans (optional)

Mix butter, sugar, eggs and flour, beating the ingredients into a nice cream. Add flavoring and nuts. Pour into greased tube pan. Bake at 300°F. for 30 minutes. Reduce heat to 275°F. and bake 45 minutes or until done. For crustier cake, add ¼ cup confectioners sugar and 1 egg to the basic recipe.

This updated version of the basic pound cake is somewhat easier than the old recipe as a cake mix is used in place of flour that has to be sifted. Regardless, it is just as appetizing.

Chocolate Pound Cake

1 box yellow cake mix ~ 1 teaspoon butter flavoring
1 carton sour cream ~ 1 cup butter-flavored oil (or regular oil)
5 eggs ~ 1 package instant chocolate pudding
1 6-ounce package chocolate chips

Mix the first five ingredients together thoroughly (cake mix, butter flavoring, sour cream, eggs, and butter-flavored oil). Add chocolate pudding and mix again. Fold in chocolate chips. Place mixture in tube pan in cold oven. Turn on oven and bake at 325°F. for one hour.

And now for a tart version of the original.

Sour Cream Pound Cake

3 cups sugar
3 cups flour
¼ teaspoon salt ~ 2 teaspoons vanilla ~ 2 sticks butter
¼ teaspoon soda ~ 6 eggs ~ 1 8-ounce tub sour cream

Cream butter and sugar then add eggs, one at a time, beating them into the mix. Sift the remaining dry ingredients (flour, salt, and soda). Add flour mixture and sour cream alternately, slowly mixing together all of the ingredients. Save the vanilla for last. Once everything is mixed place in a greased and floured tube pan and bake at 350°F. for one hour and 20 minutes.

Cream Cheese Pound Cake

This variation of the Mt. Olive Pound Cake makes it even richer. Great for special occasions.

½ pound butter ~ 1 stick margarine
1 8-ounce package creme cheese ~ 3 cups sugar
6 eggs ~ 3 cups sifted flour
1 teaspoon vanilla ~ 1 teaspoon lemon flavoring

Take butter, oleo, cream cheese, and sugar and mix into a fluffy cream. Alternate adding the eggs and flour; 2 eggs and 1 cup flour, then 1 cup flour and 2 eggs, finally 2 eggs and last cup flour. Next add flavoring. Grease and flour tube pan. Pour mixture into pan and bake at 325°F. for 40 minutes, then 300°F. for 50 minutes. Let cool in pan before removing.

Alicia's Berry Surprise Pie

2 cups berries
1½ cup sugar
½ cup nuts ~ 2 eggs
1 cup flour, sifted
¼ cup butter, melted
cooking oil
lemon juice

Grease well a 10-inch pie pan. Spread berries on the bottom of the pan and sprinkle nuts and ¾ cup sugar on top of berries. Sprinkle a little lemon juice on top of this. In a bowl, beat eggs (by hand) and remainder of sugar, flour, butter, and oil. Pour this over berries and bake at 325°F. for about 1 hour.

Blueberry Crunch

2 cups crushed pineapple ~ 1 cup sugar
1 stick margarine ~ 3 cups blueberries
1 box yellow cake mix ~ 1 cup nuts

Grease oblong pan and pour in pineapple. Add berries and ½ cup sugar. Pour in cake mix. Melt margarine and pour over cake mix. Sprinkle on nuts and remaining sugar. Bake at 350°F. for 35 to 40 minutes.

Blueberry Pineapple Surprise

1 large can crushed pineapple
1 box yellow cake mix
1 cup chopped pecans ~ 1 cup sugar
3 cups fresh or frozen blueberries
1 stick margarine, melted

Grease a 9 x 13-inch pan. Spread undrained pineapple in the bottom of the pan. Add a layer of blueberries and ½ cup of the sugar. Sprinkle dry cake mix over blueberry-sugar layer. Drizzle margarine over all and top with pecans and remainder of sugar. Bake at 350°F. for 35 to 40 minutes. After 25 minutes cut with a spoon down through all in many places to let juice come up through the cake.

Chocolate Biscuits of Doom

½ cup butter ~ ¼ cup castor sugar
1 cup self rising flour ~ Pinch salt
¼ cup chocolate powder (cocoa)

Cream butter and sugar. Sift and stir flour, salt, and cocoa into creamed mixture. Roll into balls and place on greased cooking sheet with room to spread. Flatten each ball with a fork dipped in cold water. Don't crisscross. Bake at 375°F. For 7 to 8 minutes.

Cocoa Angel Cake

¾ cup cake flour ~ ¼ cup cocoa
1¼ cups sugar ~ 10 egg whites
1 teaspoon cream of tartar
1 teaspoon vanilla ~ 1 teaspoon almond extract

Sift flour, cocoa, and ¼ of the sugar three times and set aside. Sift the remaining sugar and set aside. Gradually add cream of tartar to egg whites and beat until stiff but not dry. Fold in sugar, vanilla, and almond extract. Sift flour-cocoa mixture over batter and fold into batter. Pour into ungreased 10-inch tube pan and bake in preheated 350°F. oven for 45 minutes. Serve plain or doused with chocolate syrup and garnished with cherries.

Smoky Mountain
Death by Chocolate Cake

1 box chocolate (pudding in the box-type) cake mix
1 box (4 serving size—2 cups) instant chocolate pudding
¼ cup water ~ ½ cup sour cream ~ ½ cup oil
12 ounces semi-sweet chocolate chips

Mix all ingredients with a fork, beating 3-4 minutes until mixed well. This makes a very thick gooey mix. Pour into a greased bundt pan and bake for 55 minutes at 350°F. Cool 15 minutes before removing from the pan. No icing is necessary for this very rich cake, however, may be topped with sugar glaze. Glaze: Mix 1 box powdered sugar with ¼ cup water and a Dash of maple syrup. Drizzle over warm cake. If glaze is too thin add powdered sugar, too thick add more water.

Dessert Crêpes

3 cups flour ~ 4 eggs ~ 4 egg yolks
1 quart milk ~ 2 teaspoons sugar
½ teaspoon salt ~ 4 Tablespoons butter

Mix the flour, eggs, and egg yolks with a wire whisk. Add the milk, sugar, salt, and beat until all ingredients are thoroughly blended. Melt the butter in a small container and skim off the foam. Pour off and reserve the fat (clarified butter). Discard the sediment at the bottom of the container. Heat a skillet and brush with the clarified butter. Pour in 1 Tablespoon of the batter and tilt the pan immediately so that the batter will spread evenly over the entire base of the pan. Cook the crêpe quickly on both sides. Cook all the batter this way to make about 24 crêpes. Roll and stuff with fresh fruit, lemon juice, sugar, and/or fruit liqueurs.

Orange Slice Date Nut Loaf

2 sticks margarine ~ 4 cups plain flour
1 teaspoon soda ~ 1 cups buttermilk
1 cup dates or figs~ 1 teaspoon allspice
2 cups sugar ~ ¼ teaspoon salt ~ 4 eggs
2 cups nuts, chopped ~ 1 pound orange slice candy, chopped
1 cup brown sugar ~ ½ cup frozen orange juice

Cream margarine and sugar. Add 1 egg at a time. Mix well; add 1 cup buttermilk and soda then stir in remaining buttermilk. Add salt, dates, nuts, candy, and flour to creamed mixture. Bake in a tube pan for 2½ hours at 275°F. Mix brown sugar and orange juice and pour over hot cake.

Hot Milk Cake

4 eggs ~ 2 cups sugar ~ 2 cups flour
1 teaspoon vanilla ~ 2 teaspoons baking powder
¼ teaspoon salt ~ 1 cup milk
2 Tablespoons butter

Beat eggs until light. Add sugar and beat until creamy. Add flour, baking powder and salt. Heat milk and butter to boiling point; add to batter. Add vanilla. Bake in a 9 x 13-inch ungreased pan at 350°F. for 45 minutes.

Red Velvet Cake

2½ cups self-rising flour ~ 1 cup buttermilk
1½ cups vegetable oil ~ 1 teaspoon baking soda
1 teaspoon vanilla extract ~ ⅛ cup red food coloring
1 teaspoon unsweetened cocoa ~ 1½ cups sugar
Cocoa powder ~ 1 teaspoon white vinegar ~ 2 eggs

Heat oven to 350°F. Mix together all ingredients with an electric mixer. Spray three 9-inch round cake pan with nonstick coating. Pour batter equally into the 3 pans and bake for 20 minutes. Test for doneness with a toothpick; cool layers in pans on wire racks for 10 minutes. Carefully remove layers from pans to racks to cool completely.

Frosting:
1 stick butter, softened ~ 1½ cups cream cheese, softened
2 cups confectioners sugar ~ 2 cups chopped pecans

Combine butter, cream cheese and sugar in a bowl. Beat until fluffy then fold in 1½ cups pecans. Use to fill and frost cake when it is cool. Decorate top of cake with remaining ½ cup pecans. Refrigerate at least 1 hour before serving.

Aunt Martha's Jumbleberry Pie

2 recipes homemade pie dough

Homemade Pie Dough
1¼ cups all-purpose flour ~ Dash salt ~ 2 Tablespoons ice water
¾ stick cold unsalted butter ~ 2 Tablespoons shortening

In a large bowl blend the flour, butter (cut into bits), vegetable shortening, and salt until the mixture resembles meal. Add 2 Tablespoons ice water then toss the mixture until the water is incorporated, adding more ice water if necessary to form a dough. Form the dough into a ball, dust with flour and chill for 1 hour.

3 cups blackberries ~ ⅓ cup cornstarch
2½ cups raspberries, or boysenberries, red currants, as available
1½ cups sugar ~ ¼ cup lemon juice
⅛ teaspoon nutmeg ~ ⅛ teaspoon cinnamon
1 Tablespoon unsalted butter ~ ¼ cup half-and-half

Roll out half the dough, very thin (⅛-inch thick), on a lightly floured surface. Fit it into a 9-inch deep-dish pie plate and trim the edge, leaving a ½-inch overhang. Chill the shell while making the filling. In a large bowl toss together the berries, cornstarch, sugar, lemon juice, nutmeg, and cinnamon until the mixture is combined well. Mound the filling in the shell, and dot it with butter.

Roll out the remaining dough into a 13 to 14-inch round on a lightly floured surface. Drape it over the filling and trim leaving a 1-inch overhang. Fold the overhand under the bottom crust, pressing the edge to seal it. Crimp the edge decoratively. Brush the crust with half-and-half. Make slits in the top crust, forming steam vents, and sprinkle the pie lightly with sugar. Bake on a large baking sheet in the middle of a preheated 425°F. Oven for 20 minutes. Reduce the heat to 375°F. And bake for 35 to 40 minutes more, or until the crust is golden and the filling is bubbly. Serve with ice cream if desired.

Sherried Quinces

3 Tablespoons honey ~ 1 cup water
4 large quinces ~ ½ cup ginger, sliced
4 teaspoons cooking sherry

Peel and core quinces and cut into bite-sized pieces. Bring honey and water to a boil. Place quinces in a casserole dish. Cover with sliced ginger, sherry, and honey water. Cook with a tight fitting lid in a 350°F. oven for about 2 hours. Serve warm with freshly whipped cream.

Mississippi Mud II

2 sticks margarine or butter ~ 2 cups sugar
½ cup cocoa ~ 4 eggs ~ 1½ cups cake flour
1½ cups pecans ~ Dash of salt ~ 1 teaspoon vanilla
¾ cup miniature marshmallows

Cream butter, sugar and cocoa. Add eggs, one at a time, beating after each addition. Add flour, nuts and vanilla; mix well. Put batter in a greased and floured 13 x 9-inch pan. Bake at 325°F. for 40 minutes. Remove from oven and spread marshmallows on cake. Return to oven until marshmallows melt.

Aline's Sweet Potato Pie

1 cup mashed potatoes ~ 1½ cups sugar
1 cup evaporated milk ~ 1 teaspoon lemon flavoring
1 teaspoon vanilla flavoring ~ 3 eggs
1 stick margarine, melted ~ 2 pie shells

Mix all ingredients together and pour into pie shells. Bake at 350°F. for 40 to 45 minutes until done.

Sis' Pecan Pie V

1 cup shortening or butter ~ ½ cup sugar
3 Tablespoons flour ~ ¼ teaspoon salt
1½ teaspoon vanilla ~ ½ cup milk
1 cup chopped pecans ~ 3 eggs
1 cup corn syrup or Karo ~ 2 9-inch pie shells

Cream butter with sugar and flour. Add eggs and pecans to sugar mixture; mix well. Turn into two unbaked pie shells and bake at 325 °F. for 1 hour.

Graham Cracker Chew Bars

Bottom: 1⅓ cups fine graham cracker crumbs
2 teaspoon flour ~ ½ cup butter
Top: ⅓ cup fine graham cracker crumbs
1½ cups brown sugar ~ ½ cup broken nuts
¼ teaspoon baking powder ~ 2 well-beaten eggs
1 teaspoon vanilla

Bottom: Blend crumbs, flour, and butter with pastry blender or 2 forks until particles are size of rice. Press into greased 9-inch square pan. Bake at 350°F. for 20 minutes.
Top: Blend crumbs, sugar, nuts, and baking power. Blend in mixture of eggs and vanilla. Pour over baked bottom, spreading carefully to cover entire surface. Bake at 350°F. for 20 minutes. Let cool in pan before cutting into bars.

Banana Nut Bread

3 cups sugar ~ 1 cup butter
½ cup buttermilk ~ 3½ cups flour
2 teaspoon soda ~ 4 eggs
2 cups mashed bananas
1 cup chopped pecans

Cream sugar, butter, and eggs. Add buttermilk and dry ingredients and blend. Add bananas and pecans. Pour into well-greased and floured tube pan or 2 loaf pans. Bake at 350°F. for 1 hour and 10 minutes.

Bayou Country Spiced Muffins

1 cup soft butter or margarine
2 cups sugar ~ 1 teaspoon salt
2 eggs ~ 2 cups applesauce
3 teaspoons ground cinnamon
2 teaspoon ground allspice
1 teaspoon ground cloves
2 teaspoon baking soda ~ 4 cups flour
1 cup nuts, chopped ~ Powered sugar

Cream butter and sugar; add eggs, one at a time. Mix in applesauce and spices. Sift together salt, soda and flour. Add to applesauce mixture and beat well. Stir in nuts and bake in lightly greased miniature muffin pans at 350°F. for 8 to 10 minutes. Sprinkle with powdered sugar. Batter keeps indefinitely in refrigerator. Baked muffins freeze well; reheat before serving. Yields 7 dozen small muffins.

Date Nut Muffins

2 eggs ~ ¾ cup sugar ~ 1 teaspoon vanilla
⅛ teaspoon salt ~ ¼ teaspoon ground cinnamon
¼ teaspoon ground allspice ~ 1 cup chopped pecans
1 cup chopped dates

Stir (do not beat) eggs, sugar, and vanilla. Mix flour, salt, cinnamon, and allspice. Add pecans and dates to flour mixture. Combine the 2 mixtures. Using miniature muffin tins, grease tins well and fill half full. Bake at 325°F. for 15 minutes. Baked muffins will keep a week or more in a tin.

Blueberry Sour Cream Muffins

2 cups all-purpose flour ~ ½ teaspoon baking soda
¼ cup sugar ~ 2 teaspoons baking powder
½ teaspoon salt ~ ¼ cup cooking oil ~ ¼ cup brown sugar
2 Tablespoons all-purpose flour ~ ½ teaspoon ground cinnamon
1 egg, beaten ~ ⅓ cup milk ~ 1 cup fresh or frozen blueberries
1½ Tablespoons butter or margarine ~ 1 cup sour cream

Combine flour, baking soda, sugar, baking powder, and salt in a bowl; make a well in the center of the mixture. Combine egg, sour cream, milk, and oil; add to dry ingredients, stirring just until blended. Coat paper pan liners with cooking spray; spoon batter into liners, filling them ⅔ full. Combine brown sugar and remaining ingredients; stir until crumbly. Sprinkle over batter. Bake at 425°F. for 18 to 20 minutes.

Chapter 8
Button Poppin' Fried Favorites

When I was young just about everything was breaded and fried in lard or bacon fat. Everyone asks, "Why?" I really don't know, except to say that everything tastes so much better when it is fried. My mama is now 80+ years old and doing just fine so perhaps there is something to be said for eating everything fried in heaping spoonfuls of lard. Of all the South's fried dishes, chicken is perhaps the most familiar. That said, **Beau Catcher Chicken** is the fried chicken recipe that non-Southerner's should get to taste. It is the only kind I eat. The story goes that this recipe was handed down through the generations, moms to daughters. . . that if the daughter made this recipe just right, she'd be sure to catch that certain "beau" she'd had her eyes on. This is the recipe my mom passed down to me.

Lola's Beau Catcher Fried Chicken

1 large fryer, cut up ~ 1½ cups flour
3 Tablespoons dried minced onion ~ 1 Tablespoon Paprika
Salt and pepper to taste ~ 1 stick margarine
1 cup buttermilk
OR
1 cup milk with 2 Tablespoons vinegar and lemon juice added

Preheat oven to 375°F. Remove skin from chicken, wash, and pat dry. In a large bowl mix the dry ingredients. Put buttermilk (or milk-vinegar-lemon mixture) in a separate bowl. Melt margarine in a 9 x 12 baking pan. Dip chicken in buttermilk, then into flour mixture, then place in pan with margarine and turn over. Bake for 45 minutes to 1 hour until golden brown.

The following 18 fried recipes round out the South's favorite fried foods. If you don't see your favorite here don't worry, at the end I give instructions on how to fry just about anything!

Adeles' Corn Fritters

8¾ ounce can whole kernel corn ~ milk ~ 1 beaten egg
1½ cups sifted all purpose flour ~ ¾ teaspoon salt

Drain canned corn reserving liquid. Add enough milk to the corn liquid to make 1 cup of liquid total. Sift together dry ingredients. Combine egg, milk mixture, and corn. Add to dry ingredients, mixing until just moistened. Drop batter from Tablespoons into deep hot oil (at least 375°F.). Fry until golden brown, 3 to 4 minutes. Drain on paper towels. This recipe makes around 2 dozen, depending on how big your drops are. I usually double or triple the basic recipe. Try serving with a maple syrup "dip."

William's Country Fried Round Steak

½ to 1 pounds boneless round steak, trimmed of excess fat
1 egg, beaten ~ Grated peel and juice of 1 lemon
½ teaspoon salt ~ ½ teaspoon pepper ~ Cooking oil
½ cup fine dry bread crumbs ~ ½ cup fine cracker crumbs

Pound steak to ½-inch thickness. Cut steak into serving size pieces. Combine egg, lemon peel and juice, salt and pepper; beat well. Combine bread and cracker crumbs. Dip steak into egg mixture; dredge in crumb mixture. Cook steak cutlets in hot oil until done, turning once.

Crispy Fried Liver

1 pound baby beef liver, skin and membrane trimmed
Biscuit mix ~ Milk ~ Salt and pepper to taste

Cut in strips, 4 x 1-inch. Dip in biscuit mix, then in milk, and again in biscuit mix. Fry in hot fat over medium heat until crispy brown, about 5 minutes; turn and fry on other side. Season with salt and pepper.

Fried Cabbage

½ cup milk ~ 1 egg ~ ¾ cup cut cabbage
Salt and pepper to taste

Mix milk, egg, salt, and pepper. Chop cabbage a little large than shredded and stir into milk mixture (the more cabbage the better it is). Drop mixture by spoonfuls into a deep fryer or in vegetable oil in skillet. Fry until golden brown. Salt to taste.

Fried Egg Burgers

1 pound lean ground beef or turkey ~ 6 eggs
6 slices white bread, buttered ~ Cooking oil
Salt, pepper, and onion salt

Cut the ground beef into 6 portions then spread each buttered side of bread with 1 portion of beef. Season with salt, pepper, and onion salt to taste. Brown bread side until crisp, then fry beef side down until desired doneness. Fry eggs; season to taste. Serve with a fried egg on top hamburger; meat side up.

Angela's Fried Green Tomatoes

6 to 8 green tomatoes ~ Salt and pepper
Cooking oil, shortening, or better yet, lard
Flour or corn meal

Wash tomatoes and cut into ½ -inch slices. Roll in mixture of flour or corn meal, salt and pepper. Fry slowly in fat until brown.

This isn't exactly the same recipe that Fannie Flagg immortalized in her book "Fried Green Tomatoes at the Whistle Stop Cafe." You can add a variety of seasonings to the flour or cornmeal to dress up the basic recipe. Additionally you can, as Ms. Flagg and others have suggested a few beaten eggs to make the flour or cornmeal stick fast to the tomatoes. As kids we always liked peeling off the loose fried covering and eating it first, then getting into the meat of the tomatoes.

Fried Okra, Corn, & Tomato Surprise

1 pound fresh okra (or 1-pound bag frozen okra)
4 to 6 ears fresh corn (or 1 10-ounce box frozen corn)
1 pound canned tomatoes ~ 4 slices bacon
1 medium onion, sliced ~ 2 Tablespoons bacon grease
1 teaspoon sugar ~ Salt and pepper to taste

Wash okra, cut off stem ends, and slice in 1-2 inch slices. Cut corn off cobs. Fry bacon in heavy skillet until crisp; remove bacon. Crumble when cool. Fry onions in bacon grease until soft; add okra and cook 2 to 3 minutes, stirring occasionally. Smash tomatoes and pour them and their juice into the skillet. Add corn, bacon, and sugar. On low heat cook covered until done (about 15-20 minutes). Season to taste and serve. Turkey bacon works just as well with half or less fat. Turn this dish into an entree by leaving out the corn and serving on a bed of white rice.

Fried Fruit Pies were one of our favorite quick fried favorites as children. Today you can find a variation of this recipe at supermarket bakery counters. Today the pies are pre-made in perfect little pie shapes, then frozen for shipping across the country. They are fried frozen using deep fat donut fryers. By contrast, we took a ball of biscuit dough and stuff if with fruit, then deep fried it fresh.

Aunt Barbara's
Fried Fruit Pies

1 can plain biscuit dough
1 can fruit pie filling (any variety)
Powdered sugar for glaze (optional)

Roll out biscuit dough on a sheet of floured wax paper. Make a reservoir in the middle of each biscuit. Spoon in 1 Tablespoon of pie filling. Close up biscuit creating a crescent moon shaped roll. Be sure to pinch together sides well. Fry in deep fryer until golden brown, about 2 minutes. If sweeter pie is preferred mix 1 box of powdered sugar with water until thick, soupy consistency is achieved. Dip hot pies in glaze mix or top with whipped topping.

Fried Stuffed Hamburgers

1 pound ground beef ~ ½ teaspoon salt
Dash of pepper ~ Cooking oil
1 cup American cheese or Monterey Jack cheese, shredded
1 cup onion, finely chopped ~ 1 teaspoon barbecue sauce

Mix ground beef, salt, and dash of pepper. Between sheets of waxed paper, roll out patties ½-inch thick. Combine cheese, onion, and barbecue sauce. Place a small amount of cheese mixture in center of half of the patties. Top each with meat lids. Press around edges to seal. Fry in hot oil to desired doneness, turning once.

Oven-Baked Fried Chicken

1 cup flour ~ 1 teaspoon salt ~ ½ teaspoon pepper
2 teaspoons paprika ~ ½ cup shortening
3 pound fryer, cut in pieces

Heat oven to 425°F. Mix flour, salt, pepper, and paprika in a paper bag. Put shortening in 13 x 9-inch pan; set in oven to melt. Shake 3 or 4 pieces of chicken at a time in bag to coat thoroughly. Place chicken, skin-side down, in single layer in hot shortening. Bake 30 minutes. Turn skin-side up and bake another 30 minutes or until chicken is tender.

Carolyn's Savannah Hush Puppies

1½ cups corn meal ~ ½ cup flour
2 teaspoons baking powder ~ 1 egg
Dash salt ~ milk ~ 1 large onion, chopped fine

Mix dry ingredients together and add egg and onion. Add a little milk to the mixture, blending until pasty. Drop by teaspoon into deep, hot fat. Fry until golden brown.

In the South you'll find just about anything fried. My husband's favorite is fried sweet potatoes. But then he survived part of his childhood eating nothing but sweet potatoes. To hear his mother tell it sweet potatoes were the only substantial food that he could keep down. So how would you go about frying something like potatoes, eggplant, or fish? To fry just about *anything* put some flour seasoned with salt and pepper to your tastes in a paper bag. In a bowl beat up a couple of eggs with some milk. Dip the eggplant, sweet potatoes, fish, whatever in the egg mixture then toss in the paper bag. Shake a couple of times and fry in a skillet or deep fryer until golden brown. Use canola, peanut, vegetable, or olive oil. . . or look for lard next to the shortenings on your supermarket shelves!

Goldie's Southern Fried Chicken

½ cup milk ~ 1 egg, beaten ~ 1 cup flour
2 teaspoons salt ~ 1 teaspoon paprika
2 teaspoons black pepper ~ ½ teaspoon sage
½ teaspoon tarragon ~ 1 frying chicken, cut up
Oil, shortening, or lard for frying

Combine milk and egg and set aside. Combine flour, salt, paprika, pepper, sage, and tarragon in a paper bag. Add a few pieces of chicken at a time and shake to coat. Dip chicken in milk-egg mixture then place in bag and shake again. Heat at least ½-inch of oil in an electric frying pan or heavy skillet on medium-high heat. Brown chicken on all sides. Reduce heat to medium-low. Continue cooking until chicken is tender, about 30 to 40 minutes. Do not cover. Turn chicken several times during cooking. Drain on paper towels.

Shoestring Fried Turnips

½ cup flour ~ ¼ teaspoon salt ~ ⅛ teaspoon pepper
2 large turnips, peeled and cut unto thin strips ~ vegetable oil

Mix flour, salt, and pepper. Roll turnips in flour mixture. Fry in hot oil until golden brown. Drain on paper towels.

Denise's Squash Fritters

1 cup cooked squash ~ 1 cup flour ~ frying oil
¼ teaspoon salt ~ 1 cup onion, chopped fine
1 egg ~ ½ cup milk ~ 2 teaspoons baking powder

Mix all ingredients and form into balls. Fry in hot frying oil until golden brown.

Squash Patties

1 egg, beaten ~ 2 Tablespoons milk ~ 1 Tablespoon sugar
¼ teaspoon salt ~ 2 Tablespoons onion, chopped
1 cup cooked mashed squash ~ ½ cup self-rising flour

Mix all ingredients together and drop by Tablespoons into hot oil.
Fry until golden brown.

Tallahassee Hush Puppies

2 cups corn meal ~ 2 teaspoons baking powder
1 teaspoon salt ~ 1½ cups milk ~ ½ cup water
1 large onion, chopped fine ~ deep fat or frying oil

Sift dry ingredients together and add milk and water. Stir in the
chopped onion. With your hands, mold pieces of the dough into
pones (oblong cakes about 5 x 3 x ½ -inches). Fry in deep fat or oil
until well browned.

Zucchini Fritters

2 cups zucchini, grated ~ 2 eggs, beaten
1 teaspoon salt ~ Dash of pepper ~ 1 cup flour
½ cup parsley, chopped ~ ½ cup grated Parmesan cheese
4 Tablespoons onion, chopped ~ fat for frying

Mix zucchini and eggs, salt, pepper, parsley, onion, and cheese.
Add as much flour as needed to form fritters which will hold shape
when dropped in hot, shallow fat (up to 1 cup). Brown on both
sides. Drain on paper towels. Serve hot.

Chapter 9
Bayou to Bay Seafood Favorites

The Southern United States is delineated primarily by water, as I explained in the introduction to this book. Other than the Mason-Dixon line our boundaries consist primarily of rivers, bays, bayous, inlets, the Atlantic Ocean and the Gulf of Mexico. Its no wonder that we seem to love seafood so much and that our homemade recipes have become so incorporated into American pop-cuisine. In the Deep South catfish is considered a food group, not seafood. Look in Chapter 4 for catfish recipes. Included here are all the other seafood specialities that help to define the Southern style of cooking.

Blackened Fish

Fish fillets ~ Lemon juice
Season salt ~ Cajun fish seasoning
Non-stick spray

Rub fillets with lemon juice, season salt, and Cajun seasoning. Spray nonstick frying pan with non-stick spray. Cook fillets until tender to touch.

Clams

Deviled Clams

1 dozen clams, chopped in blender (without juice)
1 cup bread crumbs ~ 1 cup milk
1 Tablespoon butter ~ 1 small onion, grated
Pinch of parsley ~ 1 egg yoke
Dash nutmeg, salt, and pepper ~ Dash of cayenne pepper

Put butter and onion in a pan and sauté until light brown. Put in clams, bread crumbs and milk. Boil about 15 minutes. Thin out a little with clam juice. Add seasonings. Cook 5 minutes. Add egg yolk and stir quickly to keep egg from cooking. Bake in buttered clam shells (dot with extra butter). Bake at 425°F. for about 20 minutes or until golden brown. If clam juice is strong tasting or looks real "cloudy," thin out mixture with milk instead of clam juice. Don't get too thin, just about the consistency of oatmeal.

Clam Spaghetti

1½ cups minced clams ~ 1½ sticks butter
3 cloves garlic, crushed ~ 1 teaspoon oregano
1 teaspoon Italian seasoning ~ 2 teaspoons olive oil
2 cups small shell pasta ~ Parsley ~ Parmesan cheese

Cook pasta in salted boiling water. Drain and set aside. In a medium saucepan, melt butter over low heat. Add garlic, oregano, and Italian seasoning. Simmer 10 to 15 minutes. Add clams, olive oil, and pasta. Stir gently over heat until warmed through. Garnish with parsley and Parmesan cheese.

Crab

Maryland Crab Cakes

1 pound Crab Meat ~ 1 cup seasoned bread crumbs
1 large egg ~ ¼ cup mayonnaise
Salt and pepper to taste ~ 1 teaspoon Worcestershire sauce
1 teaspoon dry mustard ~ oil for frying

Remove all cartilage from crabmeat. In a bowl, mix bread crumbs, eggs, mayonnaise, and seasonings. Add crab meat and mix gently but thoroughly. If mixture is too dry, add a little more mayonnaise. Shape into 6 cakes. Cook cakes in a frying pan, in just enough oil to prevent sticking, until they are browned (about 5 minutes on each side). May also be deep-fried at 350°F. For 2-3 minutes until golden brown.

Crab Stuffed Louisiana Style

½ cup margarine ~ 1 onion, finely chopped
1 rib celery, chopped ~ ½ bell pepper, chopped
1 pound crab meat ~ 2 Tablespoons minced parsley
3 Tablespoons minced green onion, bulbs only
Salt and pepper to taste ~ 2 teaspoons lemon juice
1 teaspoon Worcestershire sauce ~ ¼ cup milk
½ teaspoon Tabasco sauce ~ 1 egg beaten (in milk)
¾ cup plain bread crumbs ~ Buttered bread crumbs
8 crab shells

Preheat oven to 400°F. Sautée onions, celery, and bell pepper in margarine until tender. Add crab meat, green onions, and parsley, and simmer about 10 minutes. Add salt, pepper, lemon juice, Worcestershire sauce, Tabasco, and egg-milk mixture. Set aside to cool slightly. Add approximately ¾ cup bread crumbs to obtain stuffing consistency. Stuff crab shells and top with buttered bread crumbs. Bake 15 minutes, or until lightly browned.

South Beach Crab Salad with Plantain and Avocado

1 pound of jumbo lump crab meat, cartilage removed
¼ cup diced red, yellow, and green bell pepper
2 green onions, finely chopped ~ ¼ cup mayonnaise
¼ cup ketchup ~ 1 yellow tomato, peeled and diced
1 red tomato, peeled and diced ~ 1 lime, juiced
Salt and Pepper to taste ~ Plantain chips ~ Sliced avocado

In a large bowl add all ingredients until blended, being careful not to shred crab meat. Serve in a mound on a chilled plate, garnish with plantain chips and sliced avocados.

One of Louisiana's most sought out dishes is Crawfish Étoufée. My aunt Lily-Belle lived on Napoleon Ave. In New Orleans for most of her life. This is her spin on the City's favorite seafood. Note that étouffant refers to sultry, suffocating temperatures (much like a 9-month New Orleans summer). While the derivation, étoufée, means a thick stew or gravy. Pronounced "ay-too-tay" in Louisiana, it is most often served over steamed rice.

Crawfish Étoufée

½ cup butter ~ 1 cup chopped green onions
¼ cup chopped parsley ~ 2 pounds crawfish tails
1 cup crawfish fat, if available, or 1 cup butter
Salt and pepper to taste
1 teaspoon cornstarch ~ Lemon slices

Melt butter in a large skillet or Dutch oven and sauté green onions until tender (about 10-15 minutes). Add parsley, crawfish tails, crawfish fat (or butter), salt, and paper to taste. Cook over medium heat 15 to 20 minutes. If a thicker étoufée is desired, dissolve cornstarch in a small amount of water and add to sauce. Serve over steamed rice and garnish with lemon slices, if desired.

Flaming Fish

4 fish fillets (Flounder, Mullet, Trout, Bass as available)
Lemon-onion baste:
½ cup lemon juice ~ Salt and pepper to taste
¼ teaspoon sugar ~ ⅛ cup green onions
2-3 ounces rum or cognac
Herbs as available (rosemary, dill, thyme, sage)

Combine the ingredients of the lemon-onion baste and mix thoroughly. Grill fillets over a medium heat, basting twice on each side with the lemon-onion baste. Cook 5-8 minutes on each side, turning once. Cover a hot platter with herbs and place fillets on it from the grill. Sprinkle herbs on top of the fillets. Pour rum over fillets and ignite. The herbs will give the fish a subtle irresistible flavor. Serve with a wild rice mix and a plate of cut raw vegetables. Try this dish outside before attempting it on guests!

Flounder

Southern Fried Flounder

1 cup flour ~ ½ teaspoon pepper
1½ teaspoon instant minced onion ~ 1 teaspoon salt
1 pound frozen flounder fillets, thawed
1 Tablespoon onion juice ~ cooking oil

Mix flour, onion, salt, and pepper in a paper bag. Sprinkle fish with onion juice and shake well in paper bag with flour mixture. Fry in about ⅛-inch hot oil until golden brown, turning once.

Luella's Spicy Stuffed Flounder

1 pound flounder fillets ~ ¼ cup minced onion
4 Tablespoons margarine ~ 10 ounces imitation crab, diced
½ cup mixed stuffing mix ~ 2 Tablespoons parsley
Salt and pepper to taste ~ ½ teaspoon Creole seasoning
Sauce:
3 Tablespoons margarine ~ 3 Tablespoons flour
dash salt ~ 1¼ cups milk ~ Paprika
1 cup shredded cheddar cheese

In saucepan, sauté onions in margarine until tender and clear but not brown. Add imitation crab meat, stuffing, parsley, salt, pepper, and Creole seasoning. Stir to mix, then remove from heat. Spoon stuffing mixture over fillets and wrap ends under, creating a roll. Place seam side down in a rectangular baking dish. **Sauce:** In a medium saucepan, melt margarine and stir in flour salt. Add milk and cook over medium heat, stirring often, until thick. Pour sauce over fillets and bake uncovered at 400°F. for 20-30 minutes or until fish flakes easily with a fork. Sprinkle with shredded cheese and paprika and bake a few minutes longer until cheese is melted.

Vegetable Stuffed Flounder

1 small zucchini ~ 1 small red pepper ~ 2 cups stuffing mix
½ cup water, hot ~ ¼ cup chicken broth
¼ cup butter, melted ~ ½ teaspoon tarragon leaves
⅛ teaspoon paprika ~ 4 flounder fillets

Cut zucchini and red pepper into thin strips. Combine vegetables, stuffing mix, water, chicken broth, tarragon, and 2 Tablespoons butter; let stand 5 minutes. Spoon and press stuffing into half of each fillet. Fold fillet over stuffing. Mix remaining butter and paprika; brush on fillets. Place in baking dish; cover and bake at 400°F. for 20 to 25 minutes or until fish flakes easily with fork.

Lobster

Louise's Lobster and Apple Bisque

1 2-pound Florida lobster ~ 3 Tablespoons olive oil
1 medium yellow onion, chopped ~ 1 carrot peeled and chopped
1 stalk celery, chopped ~ ½ cup tomato paste
2 pounds apples (your choice as available), peeled and chopped
¼ cup plum cooking wine ~ ¼ cup white port cooking wine
2 Tablespoons grated ginger ~ 2 cloves garlic, finely chopped
2 green onions, trimmed and chopped
1 Tablespoon whole black peppercorns
1 teaspoon cayenne pepper ~ 1 quart chicken stock
2 Tablespoons unsalted butter ~ 2 Tablespoons flour
2 cups heavy cream ~ Salt to taste ~ Juice of one lime

Preheat oven to 400°F. Clean lobster and rinse, retaining claws and tail in shell. Heat ½ of olive oil in a large pan over medium-high heat. Sauté lobster tails and claws (in shells) for about 3 minutes or until pieces start to turn red. Place sauté pan in preheated oven and cook lobster for about 7 minutes. Remove lobster from oven and let cool enough to handle. Pull all lobster meat from claws and tails. Do not discard shells. Cut lobster meat into a fine dice and reserve. Heat second ½ olive oil in a large saucepan over medium-high heat and sauté onion, carrot, and celery for 4 minutes or until onion is transparent, not brown. Add lobster shells and tomato paste to sauce pan. Cook for 4 minutes. Add apples, optional wine, ginger, and garlic. Cook for 8 minutes or until liquid has evaporated, stirring occasionally. Lower heat as liquid reduces, being careful not to burn solid ingredients. Add green onions, peppercorns, cayenne, cooking wine, and stock. Bring soup to a simmer and cook for 1 hour. Strain soup through a medium sieve into a large, clean pot. Return to heat, blend butter and flour and whisk into the soup, then simmer for 20 minutes. Stir in cream. Season to taste with salt and lime juice. Remove from heat then strain again. Add lobster meat and heat through. Serve in warm, flat soup bowls.

Lobster and Roasted Corn Chowder

4 ears fresh sweet Zellwood corn (if available) brushed with
butter and grilled until toasted on all sides (about 2 cups corn)
2 Tablespoons unsalted butter ~ 1 large onion, diced
2 celery stalks, diced ~ 1 leek, split, and diced
1 red bell pepper, diced ~ 3 jalapeño peppers, diced
Salt and pepper to taste ~ 1½ quarts chicken stock
1 2-pound lobster, tail hacked into sections, claws cracked,
body wrapped in cheesecloth ~ ½ cup strawberry cream

Cut the roasted corn off of cobs, reserving the corn cobs. Melt the
butter in a large, heavy bottomed soup pot. Add the corn, onion,
celery, leek, and peppers and sauté until the vegetables are soft, but
not browned. Add salt and pepper to taste and the chicken stock
and bring to a boil. Reduce to a simmer and add the reserved corn
cobs along with the lobster body. Cook 45 minutes, remove the cobs
and the lobster body. Add the hacked lobster and simmer for 4 to
5 minutes before stirring in the strawberry cream. Serve warm.

Mullet

The name "mullet" is used to identify many
fish that are not mullets at all—such as the
highly prized red mullet, which actually
belongs to the goatfish family. True
Southern mullet belong to the gray mullet
family and are available in the South as
striped or silver mullet. These silver-gray
fish are perhaps the South's second favorite
fish (after catfish). Mullet have firm white
flesh with a mild, nut-like flavor. They can
be found year round in most of the Gulf
Coast states. Try these mullet delights on
your family and tell them its bass or trout. I
bet they won't know the difference!

Stuart's Mullet Stew

3 pounds mullet ~ 8 garlic cloves ~ Juice of 1 lemon
Salt and pepper to taste ~ 2 sprigs parsley ~ 8 tomatoes, chopped
2 cups squid, and/or ~ 2 cups octopus
½ pound shrimp ~ 2 Tablespoons olive oil

Gut and clean mullet. Fillet the fish, devein and behead the shrimp, and cut the squid and octopus into pieces. Reserve the heads and the bone. In a large pot bring 6 quarts water to a boil with the tomatoes, fish bones and heads, and shrimp heads. Cook for 2 hours, then cool and pass through a fine sieve. Bring this poaching liquid back to a simmer and start adding the fish one at a time, in order of cooking time. First the squid and/or octopus, then the shrimp, and finally the mullet. Cook until all the fish are done (about 45 minutes). Mash the garlic and parsley together, then add them to the fish stew along with salt and pepper to taste. Cook another 15 minutes then remove the stew from heat. Add lemon juice and mix well. Place stew in a large serving platter and serve with a toasted country bread.

Low Country Mullet

2 pounds mullet ~ 1½ ounces parsley ~ 1 celery stalk
2 garlic cloves ~ 2 Tablespoons flour ~ Salt and pepper to taste
Olive oil ~ 1 pound ripe tomatoes, peeled and chopped

Clean and fillet the mullet. Mince parsley, celery, and garlic and sauté in a sauce pan with oil. When the celery is tender add the tomatoes and cook for 10 minutes. Remove from heat and set aside. Coat the fish with flour and brown them in oil until golden brown on both sides. Add salt and pepper to taste. Grease a casserole with oil, place the mullets in it and pour the sauce in the casserole with the fish. Bake for 10 minutes at 400°F. Serve with a generous sprinkling of chopped parsley.

Mullet Festival
Mullet in Vine Leaves

This simple recipe comes from the famed Northwest Florida Mullet Festival held annually in Niceville, Florida. Yes, mullet have their own Southern festival. This recipe shows you how to prepare mullet on your backyard grill. In fact, just about any fish can be prepared this way on the grill. The simplicity of this recipe shows that many fish need little more than delicate flavoring and seasoning to be delicious! Vine leaves may be hard to find. The adventurous Southern cook may trudge into nearby woods for any number of Southern vines that work just as well as the Mediterranean variety found in specialty food stores. Banana leaves work equally well as do corn husks. The presentation, wrapped in leaves, will impress your family and guests alike.

4 mullet, gutted, scales and fins removed
1 lemon, thinly sliced ~ 1 bunch fresh dill or thyme
2 Tablespoons olive oil ~ Salt and pepper to taste
1 pack vine leaves (if not available use foil)

Wash the fish thoroughly and dry with kitchen paper. Push some of the lemon slices and hers into each belly cavity and sprinkle with oil and seasoning. Rub the outsides of the fish with oil, sprinkle with seasoning, then wrap in vine leaves (or foil) to cover completely. Leave in a cool place. Lightly oil a barbecue grill. Cook fish on grill for about 5 minutes on each side, turning occasionally, until the leaves are charred and the fish feels firm when pressed. When fish are done, the skin will peel away with the charred vine leaves and the flesh will be firm and opaque.

Oysters

Cheesed Oysters

1 16-ounce package cheese crackers
½ teaspoon paprika ~ ¼ teaspoon rubbed oregano
oil, for deep frying ~ 2 eggs ~ Tarter sauce
2 Tablespoons water ~ 1 pint oysters
Lemon wedges ~ Dill pickles

Crush crackers into very fine crumbs between waxed paper. Mix with paprika and oregano and set aside. Beat eggs with water. Dip oysters into eggs and roll in crumbs. Lay on a flat surface at least 30 minutes to set crust. Fry in oil until crusty, about 4 to 5 minutes. Drain on paper towels. Garnish with lemon and dill pickles. Serve with tarter sauce.

Deviled Oysters

1 pint oysters in liquid ~ ¼ cup butter, melted
1 cup oyster crackers, crushed
1 medium bell pepper, seeded and chopped
¼ cup parsley, chopped ~ 1 medium onion, grated
2 teaspoons Worcestershire sauce
2 hard-boiled eggs, chopped ~ 3 eggs, lightly beaten
½ cup light cream ~ 1 teaspoon Dijon mustard
⅛ teaspoon cayenne pepper ~ ½ teaspoon salt

Combine all ingredients and toss to mix well. Turn into a buttered 5-6 cup casserole dish. Bake 30 minutes at 375°F. Until set and lightly browned. For individual servings, spoon mixture into buttered scallop shells and bake for 15 minutes. To serve as hors d'oeuvres, bake in butter oyster or clam shells for 10 minutes or until set.

Red Snapper

Key Largo Snapper

3-4 cups ripe tomatoes, chopped (about 10)
1 cup red onion diced ~ ¼ cup yellow pepper, chopped
1 cup zucchini, quartered lengthwise and sliced
3 cloves garlic, minced ~ 1½ teaspoons oregano
3 small red chilies, crushed ~ 3 Tablespoons olive oil
2 limes, cut in wedges ~ 1½ teaspoons balsamic vinegar
1 bunch cilantro leaves, chopped ~ Salt to taste

Preheat broiler while making sauce. In a large skillet, heat the oil over medium heat and sauté the garlic, onions, and yellow pepper for 2 minutes. Add the oregano and sauté for another 2 minutes as the onions just begin to brown. Add the tomatoes, chilies, and a dash of salt. Finally add zucchini and stir well and cover for 3 minutes more. Remove from heat, not allowing zucchini to soften. Broil snapper for 4 minutes, each side or until done. Place fish on serving platter, Douse with sauce, garnish with limes, and sprinkle with cilantro leaves.

Whole Fried Red Snapper

1½ pounds red snapper ~ 2 cups buttermilk
2 cups flour ~ Salt and pepper to taste
Rice:
2 cups cooked rice ~ 3 Tablespoons basil chopped
1 stick butter ~ Juice of 1 lime
Garlic Sauce:
2 ounces olive oil ~ 3 cloves garlic, thin sliced
1 teaspoon ginger, minced ~ 3 Tablespoons cilantro
4 plum tomatoes, diced ~ 3 cups shrimp stock
Salt and Pepper to taste

For the snapper: remove the gills, air bubble lining, and scales from the fish. Cut ¼-inch deep slits vertically down the fish three times from head to tail. Season the fish well, starting from the inside out. This insures that the fish is fully seasoned. With a bamboo skewer, pierce the skin through the back of the head, push the skewer through. Bend the fish into a "C" shape and pierce the skin at the head of the tail and push the skewer through again to hold the fish's shape. Pour the buttermilk over the fish, making sure that the inside cavity is also reached. Flour the fish, including the inside cavity. Make sure that the fins are also floured and free from the body. Fry the fish at 350°F (head first if it won't fit in your fryer). After 8 minutes move the fish and fry the tail portion. Remove from oil and drain all oil onto a paper towel. For the rice: place butter, basil, and lime juice in a food processor. Allow the butter to soften before pureeing. Puree for thirty seconds to a minute, until a nice green color is achieved. Melt 3 Tablespoons of the mixture in a sauté pan. Add rice and reheat and season. For the garlic sauce: Heat the oil over a medium heat, adding the garlic and slowly sautéing until golden brown and crispy. Add the ginger, cilantro, and tomatoes and sauté until fragrant. Add the shrimp stock and reduce for one minute after a boil is reached. Place the rice in the center of serving platter with the sauce around the rice. Place the fish in the center of the bed of rice, standing vertical.

Salmon

You might not think of salmon as a Southern fish and in reality it isn't. I don't know of anywhere in the South where they spawn naturally. However, it was often the only protein that we got during some of the toughest times in the 1940s. It could always be found canned. Often the government distributed it free to residents of our impoverished area of Mississippi. Therefore there are plenty of homespun Southern salmon recipes that have been handed down for going on three generation. This one is my favorite.

My sisters and I all had board-straight hair when we were young. We all wanted curly hair like the movie stars we'd see on Saturdays at the 5¢ matinee. Our brothers convinced us that if we ate the burnt salmon patties that our hair would curl just like the stars we so emulated back then. Needless to say we ate a lot of burnt salmon patties and our hair did not curl. Today their advice about curly hair and canned salmon are one of my fondest memories of our childhood. I still make this recipe and I make sure to burn a few, just for myself.

Salmon Patties

2 cups canned pink salmon ~ 1 egg
⅓ cup minced onion ~ ½ cup flour
1½ teaspoons baking flour ~ 1½ cups shortening

Drain salmon; then set aside 2 Tablespoons of the juice. In a medium mixing bowl mix salmon, egg, and onion until sticky. Stir in flour and add baking powder to salmon juice; stir into salmon mixture. Form into small patties and fry until golden brown, about 5 minutes, in hot shortening. Serve with tarter sauce or Caesar salad dressing.

Scallops with Caramelized Cauliflower

½ cup water ~ ½ cup raisins ~ ½ cup capers (optional)
1 Tablespoon sherry vinegar ~ Grated nutmeg
Salt and cayenne pepper ~ 2 Tablespoons butter
½ head of cauliflower, sliced into ¼-inch thick pieces
12 large sea scallops

In a small saucepan, cook water, raisins, and optional capers until raisins are plump (about 5 minutes). Pour mixture into blender and add vinegar, nutmeg, salt, and pepper. Blend until smooth. Set sauce aside. In a sauté pan, heat butter and sauté cauliflower until golden on both sides. To prevent cauliflower from burning add about 1 Tablespoon of water to the pan while cooking. Set cauliflower aside. In a third pan, sauté sea scallops in a small amount of butter, about 1½ minutes on each side. To serve, place 3 scallops on each plate, top with cauliflower, and finish with the raisin emulsion.

Wally's Mak Nuggets (Shark)

Mako (or any available) shark
cut into 1½-inch cubes
Garlic powder ~ Bread crumbs ~ Oil ~ Parmesan cheese
Parsley ~ Salt and pepper ~ 1 Tablespoon Hot sauce

Mix together 2 parts bread crumbs with 1 part Parmesan cheese. Add parsley, garlic powder, and salt and pepper to taste. Place shark in oil, Hot sauce, then roll in bread crumbs mixture until covered. Place coated shark on barbecue grill prepared with oil. Grill for no more than 90 seconds on each side, turning carefully. Serve as appetizers.

Seafood Gumbo

1 gallon water for boiling sausage ~ 1 quart water for roux
1 pound andouille (chitterlings), cut into 4-6-inch lengths
1 pound smoked port sausage, cut into 4-6-inch lengths
8 large chicken breasts, boned, skinned, halved, well-seasoned
1 cup vegetable oil ~ 1½ cups flour
1 cup finely-chopped onion ~ 3 shallots, finely chopped
1-2 Tablespoons chopped parsley
1 14½-ounce can chicken broth
1-2 pints oysters, drained, liquid reserved

In a large pot, gently boil andouille in 1 gallon of water for 30 minutes. Add smoked sausage and continue to boil for 15 minutes more. Remove from heat and cool, reserving stock.

In a large, heavy pot, make a brown sauce (roux) with flour and oil. When roux is dark brown, add chicken pieces. Over medium heat, brown chicken on both sides for about 15 minutes. In center of pot, push chicken aside and add onions. Cook over low heat until onions are clear, stirring occasionally. While onions are cooking, heat 1 quart of water. When onions are clear, gradually add water, reserved stock, and chicken broth. Bring to a boil. Stir to mix thoroughly and reduce heat to simmer. Cover and cook 45 minutes.

Cut cooled andouille and sausage into bite-sized pieces. At the end of the 45-minute cooking time, add sausage pieces, andouille, shallots, and parsley. Cook an additional 15 minutes. Oyster liquid can be added to taste. Oysters should be dropped in just before serving, cooking just until curled. If gumbo is to be frozen, add oysters when thawed and reheated. Serve over steamed rice.

Shrimp

Creole Shrimp

2 pounds shrimp ~ 1 large onion diced
4 Tablespoons cooking fat ~ 1 can tomatoes (2 cups)
1½ teaspoon, parsley ~ 1 clove garlic
Salt and pepper to taste ~ 2 Tablespoons flour
1 bay leaf ~ Celery salt to taste
1 lemon, sliced ~ Dash of red pepper

Brown onion and flour in fat. Add shrimp, cooking until shrimp turn pink and slightly brown, stirring constantly. Add tomatoes and remaining ingredients and bring to boil. Cover and lower heat to a simmer for 30 minutes. Serve over rice.

Hot Shrimp Salad

1 small can shrimp, drained ~ 2 cups chopped cooked chicken
1 cup mayonnaise ~ 2 Tablespoons chopped green onions
1 cup chopped celery ~ 1 small jar pimento, drained
1 can cream of chicken soup ~ 1 Tablespoon lemon juice
½ teaspoon salt ~ 1 cup uncooked rice
¼ cup slivered almonds

Cook rice and mix with other ingredients. Top with bread crumbs and bake in 13 x 9 x 2-inch baking dish at 350°F. about 20 minutes.

Darla's Louisiana Shrimp

1 pound large shrimp, beheaded, peeled, and deveined
¼ stick butter ~ ½ cup chopped onions
¼ pound sliced mushrooms ~ ½ teaspoon salt
1 Tablespoon cornstarch ~ Cayenne pepper (optional)
1 teaspoon Worcestershire Sauce ~ ¼ cup water

Melt butter in skillet. Sauté onion and mushrooms over medium heat until soft. Add shrimp and cook, stirring occasionally until shrimp turns pink. Dissolve cornstarch in water and add to skillet along with salt, Worcestershire sauce, and cayenne, if desired. Stir over low heat until sauce thickens. Serve over thin noodles or rice.

Spanish Style Garlic Shrimp
with Ham and Bell Pepper

2 pounds large shrimp (about 28), deveined and shelled,
leaving the tail and the first joint of the shell intact
1½ teaspoons salt ~ 8 garlic cloves, sliced thin
½ cup olive oil ~ ¼ pound thick-sliced cooked ham, chopped
¼ teaspoon dried hot red pepper flakes
1 red bell pepper, chopped ~ ⅓ cup cooking sherry
Minced parsley leaves ~ Crusty bread

Rinse the shrimp and pat them dry. Sprinkle the shrimp on both sides with salt. In a large skillet cook the garlic in oil over moderate heat, stirring until it is golden. Remove and set aside. Add the ham and red pepper flakes to the skillet and cook the mixture, stirring, for 5 minutes, or until the ham deepens in color. Add the bell pepper and cook the mixture, stirring, until the bell pepper is softened. Add the shrimp and sauté the mixture over moderately high heat, turning the shrimp frequently, for 3 minutes. Add the sherry and the cooked garlic and simmer the mixture until the shrimp are just cooked through. Serve shrimp mixture on a heated serving dish, sprinkle it with parsley, and serve with a crusty bread.

Swordfish

Fettuccine with Swordfish
and Snap Beans

12 ounces snap beans, snapped ~ 2 cups matchstick cut carrots
8 ounces fettuccine ~ 2 teaspoons oil
1 pound skinless swordfish steaks, cut into ¾-inch cubes
3 Tablespoons parsley, chopped ~ 1 Tablespoon flour
½ cup bottled clam juice ~ ½ cup chicken broth (canned)
½ cup white wine (optional) ~ Juice of 1 lemon
4 green onions, sliced thin ~ Paprika ~ Lemon wedges

Blanch snap beans in a medium saucepan of boiling salted water for 1 minute. Add carrots and blanch 1 minute longer. Drain. Rinse under cold water and drain again. Cook fettuccine in a large pot of boiling salted water until pasta is tender but still firm to bite. Meanwhile, heat oil in a large nonstick skillet over high heat. Sprinkle fish with salt and pepper. Add fish to skillet and sauté until golden brown and almost cooked through, about 2 minutes. Using slotted spoon transfer fish to plate. Tent with foil to keep warm. Add parsley and flour to skillet, stir for 30 seconds. Add clam juice, broth, optional wine, and lemon juice. Simmer until sauce thickens, stirring constantly, about 2 minutes. Add snap beans and carrots and simmer another minute. Add fish and stir gently until heated through, about 1 minute. Drain pasta. Divide among 4 plates. Spoon fish, vegetables and sauce over pasta. Sprinkle with green onions and paprika. Garnish with lemon wedges.

Swordfish Pico de Gallo

2 large tomatoes, diced ~ 1 green onion bunch, thinly sliced
2 jalapeño chilies, seeded, diced ~ 2 Tablespoons olive oil
Salt and Pepper to taste

Combine in bowl. Serve with Swordfish tacos (next recipe).

Swordfish Tacos

1 pound ¾-inch-thick swordfish steaks
Olive oil ~ Warm corn tortillas
Lime wedges ~ Cabbage, sliced thinly
Pico de Gallo (previous recipe) ~ Sour cream

Prepare barbecue (medium-high heat) or preheat broiler. Brush swordfish generously with olive oil and season with salt and pepper. Grill or broil until just cooked through, about 4 minutes per side. Transfer steaks to plate and cut into chunks. Serve swordfish with corn tortillas, lime wedges, cabbage, Pico de Gallo, and sour cream, allowing guests to assemble their own tacos.

Grilled Swordfish
with Salsa

¾ cup diced, peeled cucumber
6 Tablespoons chopped red onion
3 Tablespoons chopped fresh mint
1 Tablespoon white wine vinegar
2½ teaspoons olive oil ~ 1½ teaspoons sugar
2 6-7-ounce swordfish steaks
cut about 1-inch thick
Your favorite homemade salsa

Combine cucumber, onion, mint, vinegar, oil, and sugar in a medium bowl. Toss to blend. Season with salt and pepper to taste. Prepare barbecue grill or preheat broiler. Brush swordfish with remaining 1 teaspoon oil and season with salt and pepper. Grill or broil swordfish until just opaque in the center, about 4 minutes per side. Place swordfish on plates and top with favorite salsa.

Trout Stuffed Tomatoes

1 pound smoked trout ~ 1 egg, beaten
6 large tomatoes ~ Dash pepper
1 teaspoon salt ~ 1 cup cooked rice
¾ cup grated cheese ~ 1 Tablespoon melted butter
¼ cup dry bread crumbs

Wash tomatoes, removing stem ends, and centers. Sprinkle with salt. Coarsely flake the fish. Combine the rice, cheese, egg, and smoked fish. Season to taste with salt and pepper. Fill the tomatoes with trout mixture and place in a well-greased baking dish. Add the melted butter to the bread crumbs, mix and sprinkle over the top of tomatoes. Bake in a 350°F. Oven for 25-30 minutes or until tomatoes are tender. Serve on crisp lettuce leaves.

Tuna Casserole

¼ pound pasta ~ ½ cup mayonnaise or salad dressing
½ cup milk ~ 1 can condensed cream soup, mushroom or celery
1 cup American cheese, shredded ~ ½ teaspoon dry mustard
1 cup canned tuna ~ 1 cup soft bread crumbs
2 Tablespoons butter, melted

Cook pasta according to package directions; drain and set aside. Combine mayonnaise with milk. Stir in soup, cheese, and mustard. Gently stir in the cooked pasta and drained tuna. Pour into 1½ quart casserole. Bake at 350°F. for 30 minutes. Combine bread crumbs and butter and sprinkle over casserole. Bake 5 additional minutes.

I can think of hundreds of other great Southern seafood dishes that I'd like to include but they'll have to wait for another book. Next I recall our favorite **Southern Holidays**. Christmas, Mardi Gras, Easter, and Thanksgiving meals and delights are all shared in Chapter 10.

Chapter 10
Southern Holidays

It's not true that Southern's celebrate more holidays than the rest of the country. It just seems that way. We have a way of taking just about any day and making it a special occasion. One of my sons' makes his birthday last most of the month of July, every year. And no, he's not a toddler. At this writing he's pushing 40. Its just that he was raised in the Southern tradition of taking life a little easier than the rest of the country.

Christmas is certainly the biggest and most elaborate of Southern Holidays. After Christmas there is Mardi Gras which is now celebrated in many locales across the Southern Gulf Coast. Next we celebrate Easter, and finally there is Thanksgiving. The other holidays are not really big Southern events so I leave them for you to imagine yourself. Here I begin with my favorite of all holidays, Christmas.

There are many Christmases that I remember, good and bad. Christmas has over the years taken on a treble significance for me. I was not only born on Christmas Day but I was married, another Christmas Day, twenty years later.

My mama always jokes that I was born on Christmas because she ate too much turkey dinner that day. Chances are that wasn't the whole truth. We were so poor in those days that I doubt there was enough for anyone to eat "too" much of. Even more suspect is that fact that none of my family can ever remember even seeing a turkey, much less eating one in Mississippi before around 1970. There are other Christmases that beg a footnote in my increasingly jumbled mind. My husband says the Christmas of 1938 stands out because they had absolutely nothing to eat that year. We didn't know one another in those days even though his family's farm was just across the hollow from my own family's place. He says he remembers that it was very cold and grey. It had snowed all night Christmas Eve, a very rare occurrence in Southern Mississippi. His dad had one buckshot shell left in his shotgun and decided to see how many of the blackbirds roosting in the barn he could get with that single shell. He promised my husband and his four brothers and sisters that they would have something to eat for Christmas dinner.

As he tells the story, his dad crept into the barn while all the kids ran around to the side, leaving five pair of little tracks in the fresh snow. There a long crack in the barn's wall revealed their dad, crouched, pointing his rifle toward the blackbirds above. His sister Odessa cried, worrying about the birds' welfare while another sister, Weezy, teased her, saying that the baby blackbirds would be motherless when their daddy was through with 'em. My husband shushed them both and there, in the bitter cold, they all watched silently for what seemed an eternity as their father aimed, corrected, aimed again, and corrected agin. Finally the shot rang out and six blackbirds fell to the ground. In retrospect the birds were probably happy to leave that miserable barn not to mention the lamentably cold Mississippi winter. Meanwhile my mother-in-law had been out digging sassafras root along the country road that traversed their property. The ground was hard but not frozen solid. He says he remember her walking up the hill with a pick ax in one hand and an arm full of sassafras in the other. Her frock was covered with dirty red clay and she looked tired, and old. He says she looked older then than she did fifty years later, just before her death. They were hard times indeed but he and his siblings had blackbird and sassafras root tea that Christmas. No one went hungry.

Then there was the Christmas of 1955 that my husband and I married. It was the only day that he could leave his army post, so we hurriedly married at the little Eminence church outside of Seminary, Mississippi, only a stone's throw from our ancestral homes. But most of all we remember the good holidays, with our children, when financial considerations were no longer a worry.

Thankfully the past forty Christmases have been joyful. We've learned to eat turkey and enjoy it, though we prefer a fresh ham. We've even managed to survive the commercialization of what was once a special time when family and friends decorated their houses with boughs of berries and branches from the land. Over the years a few special recipes have become tradition. Here I bring some of those favored recipes from both good times and bad, though I'll spare you the challenge of killing, plucking, and cooking blackbird!

Around our houses at Christmastime there is always lots of food. We call them munchies, snacks, sweets, whatever. Culinarily speaking I start this chapter with three of my favorite Christmastime hor d'oeuvres. Hot and spicy Sausage Balls and Spinach Balls are always a hit, easy to make, and reflect the unique taste of Southern cooking. Christmas Pâté is something you'll only find deep in the South woods.

Hor d'oeuvres

Sausage Balls

2 cups Bisquick
1 pound hot country sausage
10 ounces (approximately) sharp cheddar cheese, grated

Mix the three ingredients together with your hands. This may take some time. Make sure the sausage is completely integrated into the flour before you washup. Once thoroughly mixed roll the mix into balls. Bake in 350°F. oven for 20 minutes (balls will achieve a nice orange tan). They'll go fast so you might want to start with a double mix.

Often people ask if they can substitute the hot sausage with something milder. Doing so robs the balls of their minor bite. It is surprising how the Bisquick tones down the hot sausage. Try it my way first, then experiment if you're not satisfied.

Spinach Balls

2 10-ounce packages frozen spinach
2 cups herb-flavored stuffing mix
1 large onion, finely chopped
6 eggs, beaten well ~ ¾ cup melted margarine
½ cup grated Parmesan cheese
¾ Tablespoon Cayenne pepper (to taste)
1½ teaspoons garlic salt
1-2 teaspoons Creole seasoning (optional)

Preheat oven to 325°F. Lightly grease a cookie sheet. Cook spinach according to package directions and drain well, squeezing to remove excess water. Combine spinach with stuffing mix, chopped onion, eggs, margarine, Parmesan cheese, Cayenne pepper, and garlic salt. Mix well. Shape into ¾-inch balls and place on cookie sheet. Bake 15-20 minutes.

Spinach Balls are successfully frozen by placing on a pan in freezer until hard, then storing in airtight bags. To serve from frozen, thaw slightly and bake 20-25 minutes on low heat (200°F.). If you don't tell anyone there is spinach in these balls they'll never know. They are so delightfully. . . different!

Christmas Pâté

8 ounces lean ground pork (or beef) ~ 8 ounces ground veal
1 medium-size yellow onion (chopped)
1 clove garlic (minced) ~ ½ cup low-fat (1%) milk
2 large egg whites ~ ½ cup fresh bred crumbs (about 1 slice)
3 sprigs parsley ~ ½ teaspoon dried oregano leaves
¼ teaspoon salt ~ ¼ teaspoon dried thyme leaves
Dash ground sage ~ Dash pepper

Preheat oven to 325°F. Line an 8 x 4 x 2-inch loaf pan with foil, extending the foil about 1 inch above the pan on all sides. Lightly grease the foil. In a nonstick skillet, cook the pork (or beef), veal, onion, and garlic over moderately high heat for 10 minutes or until browned. Drain any fat. In a food processor or blender process the pork (or beef) mixture and milk until almost smooth. Add egg whites, bread crumbs, parsley, oregano, salt, thyme, sage, and pepper. Process until almost smooth. Spread in foil-lined pan. Cover pan with foil, place it in a larger baking pan, and pour hot water around loaf pan to a depth of 1 inch. Bake for 1 hour or until a baking thermometer inserted in the center registers 170°F. Cool on a wire rack for 30 minutes. Refrigerate for at least 6 hours. Grasp the edges of the foil and lift the pâté out of the pan. Carefully remove the foil. Using a thin-bladed sharp knife, thinly slice pâté and then halve slices. Arrange pâté slices on a kale-lined plate and serve with miniature pumpernickel-rye bread.

Christmas and Thanksgiving Dinner

It's become tradition in our family to prepare a large turkey for both Thanksgiving and Christmas. The dinner begins a day of family fellowship that lasts well into the evening on both of these special days. In years past our family was spread across the globe but thankfully, we've all settled within 3 hours of one another so we try our best to get everyone around the formal dining table at least twice a year. My husband prepares all the food on these two special days. The following recipes represent his own Southern version of how to prepare for a large gathering.

Walt's Holiday Dinners

The Turkey

Walt's formula for selecting a turkey is 2 pounds per person. For our family the turkey must always be at least 20 pounds to serve a group of 10 family members. If you're serving 20; double these recipes.

1 20-pound (or larger) turkey
1 large baking bag ~ 1 teaspoon all purpose flour

Thaw the turkey until the neck bone is easily removed. Leave the turkey in the refrigerator for 24 hours to achieve at least this level of thaw. Remove the neck bone, giblets, and cut off the tail and wing tips. Wash thoroughly and drain. Dust the inside of a large cooking bag with a teaspoon of flour. Place the bag in a large baking pan and then insert the turkey in the bag, neck first.

The Giblet Broth

Turkey neck, liver, gizzards, tail, etcetera
8 chicken bouillon cubes

Boil whole (or chopped) in 2 quarts of water for 20 minutes.

Turkey Stuffing

10 cups cornbread, crumbled ~ 4 cups onion, chopped
4 cups celery, chopped ~ 2 cups bread stuffing mix
2 teaspoons poultry seasoning ~ 2 teaspoons sage
1 teaspoons black pepper ~ 2 sticks margarine, chunked
2 Tablespoons honey ~ 2 quarts hot turkey giblet broth

In a large bowl or cake pan cover mix cornbread, onion, celery, stuffing mix, and spices. Once thoroughly mixed add honey and margarine. Pour hot giblet liquid over mixture. Mix with a large spoon until margarine is thoroughly mixed into the dressing. Stuff the turkey just prior to cooking. Seal the baking bag and cook 20-25 minutes per pound in a 350°F. oven. For a 20 pound stuffed turkey the baking time would be approximately 4 hours. Test the leg area of turkey to ensure that it is done. If the leg easily separates from the body the turkey is ready.

Turkey Gravy

1 cup flour ~ ½ cup cooking oil
1 stick margarine ~ 1 cup milk ~ Salt to taste
1 teaspoon black pepper ~ 1 quart giblet broth

In a large frying pan mix cooking oil, flour, and margarine. Cook on high heat, stirring until mixture is browned. Add milk and giblet broth. Bring to a boil, stirring constantly. Reduce heat and simmer 10 minutes, adding additional giblet broth to maintain desired thickness. Add pepper and salt to taste. Add additional liquid if necessary.

Round off the Thanksgiving or Christmas dinner with sweet potatoes, green peas, collards, and horosses. Additionally, we always have mashed potatoes, hot biscuits, and cranberry sauce, recipes you can find elsewhere in this volume. For dessert divinity is a holiday time favorite. Choose several more desserts from the many sweet recipes in Chapter 7 or sample these five additional Southern holiday favorites; almond-ham rollups, divinity, Japanese fruitcake, pumpkin cake rolls, raspberry fudge cake, and sweet potato pudding.

Sweet Potatoes

4 cups sweet potatoes, canned ~ ½ cup brown sugar
1 stick margarine ~ ½ cup honey
½ cup orange juice ~ 1 teaspoon lemon juice
Paprika ~ ½ teaspoon cinnamon

Drain juice from the potatoes into a sauce pan. Stir in other ingredients and bring to a boil. Simmer for 30 to 45 minutes, stirring occasionally. About 30 minutes before serving add potatoes and simmer until spooning to plates. Garnish with paprika.

Green Peas

4 cups small green peas, fresh, frozen, or canned
½ stick margarine
Salt to taste

Place peas and juice (for frozen peas add 4 cups water) in saucepan. Add margarine and salt to taste. Bring to boil then simmer 10 minutes.

Granddaddy's Collard Greens
& Okra

3 pounds collard greens ~ 1 pound okra
1 large red onion, sliced ~ 5 cloves garlic, crushed
2 Tablespoons oil ~ 1 Tablespoon ground coriander
½ teaspoon cayenne pepper ~ ½ cup coarsely chopped cilantro

Wash collard leaves thoroughly. Stack approximately 15 leaves evenly. Roll from long side in cigar fashion. Cut int ⅛-inch ribbons. Continue until all leaves are cut. Drop into boiling water just to cover. Blanche 4 minutes. Reserve one cup cooking liquid then drain. Cut off the tops of the okra. Slice diagonally into about 4 to 5 slices per stem. Heat oil in a large skillet on medium heat. Add okra, onion, and garlic. Sauté 8 minutes. Add drained collards, coriander, and cayenne. Stir-fry on medium high heat 5 minutes. Serve with cilantro as garnish. Add some of the juices from boiling pot if desired.

Melba's Collard Greens

2 pounds fresh collard greens ~ 2 cups water
1 medium onion, chopped ~ Sugar ~ Seasonings

Soak and wash collard greens removing all grit. Remove hard stems. Place greens together in small bunches. Roll together then cut crosswise into wide strips. Place greens in water and season. Cook until soft.

Holiday Horosses

4 medium red apples ~ ⅓ cup blackberry juice
⅓ cup honey ~ ⅓ cup chopped pecans

Core apples but do not peel. Place apples in a food processor. Process on and off until chopped medium. Transfer to a large bowl. Add honey, juice, and pecans. Mix well and serve.

After Dinner Treats
Almond-Ham Rollups

1 cup cream cheese ~ 1 teaspoon Worcestershire sauce
2 Tablespoons mayo or salad dressing
1 teaspoon instant minced onion ~ ¼ teaspoon dry mustard
¼ teaspoon paprika ~ ⅛ teaspoon pepper
⅛ teaspoon hot sauce ~ ¾ pound thin sliced boiled ham
1 Tablespoon finely chopped almonds, toasted

Combine all ingredients except ham, stirring until blended. Spread 1 Tablespoon of mixture on each ham slice. Roll up jelly roll fashion starting at short end. Wrap in plastic wrap and freeze up to 1 month. Thaw at room temperature 1 hour before serving. Cut each roll into ¾-inch slices and spear with a fancy toothpick for serving.

Divinity is one of kids favorite Southern desserts. It is traditionally made only around the holidays. For more practical reasons it was probably only made then in the old days. It can be a total flop if the weather is too damp or humid as are so many Southern summers. I always color divinity green and red just for a little added holiday cheer!

Gladys' Divinity

3½ cups sugar ~ ½ cup corn syrup ~ 2 cups boiling water
3 egg whites ~ 1 teaspoon vanilla ~ Baking powder
1 cup pecans or candied fruit

Boil sugar, syrup and water until mixture makes a firm ball in cold water. Beat egg whites stiff, adding a pinch of baking powder while beating. Pour syrup very slowly over egg whites, adding another pinch of baking powder, beating all the while. Add vanilla while beating. Add the nuts or fruit, if desired. Beat until ready to drop by teaspoonfuls onto waxed paper. Note that my mother-in-law Gladys used to make this, beating with a fork!

I don't know how Japanese Fruit Cake came to be a Southern holiday favorite. I don't even know that the name has anything to do with the country or "traditional" fruit cake. The Japanese Fruit Cake looks and tastes more like a birthday cake with some nuts and raisins added for flavor. Nevertheless, true Southern cooks will always have one prepared ahead and ready for company around the holidays.

Japanese Fruit Cake

Cake:
1 cup butter ~ 1 teaspoon ground cloves
2½ cups sugar ~ 1 teaspoon ground allspice
½ cup milk ~ 1 teaspoon ground cinnamon
6 eggs, beaten ~ 2 teaspoons baking powder ~ 1 cup raisins
4 cups plain flour ~ 1 cup nuts ~ ¼ teaspoon salt

Cream butter and sugar then add milk and beat well. Add beaten eggs. Sift together dry ingredients, mixing into batter. Finally add nuts and raisins. Reserve 1¾ cups batter for filling. Bake in 3 round layer pans at 375°F. For about 25 minutes.

Japanese Fruit Cake Filling

Filling:
2 cups sugar ~ 1 cup nuts ~ 3 Tablespoons butter
1¾ cups cake batter ~ ¼ cup candied cherries
Juice and grated rind of 2 lemons ~ 1 cup water
2 cans coconut ~ 1 cup canned pineapple, drained

Combine sugar and water in a saucepan. Bring to a boil and cook until slightly syrupy. Add batter, lemon juice and rind. Cook again until thick. Once thick add nuts, melted butter, pineapple and candied fruit. Put between the layers and on top of the Japanese Fruit Cake.

Dess' Pumpkin Cake Rolls

¾ cup flour ~ 2 teaspoon cinnamon
1 teaspoon baking powder ~ 1 teaspoon ginger
½ teaspoon salt ~ ½ teaspoon nutmeg ~ 3 eggs
1 cup sugar ~ ⅔ cup canned pumpkin ~ Powdered sugar
1 teaspoon lemon juice ~ 1 cup walnuts, chopped
Filling: 6 ounces cream cheese ~ ¼ cup butter
½ teaspoon vanilla ~ 1 cup powdered sugar

Stir together flour, cinnamon, baking powder, ginger, salt and nutmeg. In a small mixing bowl beat eggs with mixer on high speed about 5 minutes or until thick and lemon-colored. Gradually add sugar, beating until sugar dissolves. Stir in pumpkin and lemon juice. Fold dry ingredients into pumpkin mixture. Spread in greased and lightly floured 15 x 10 x 1-inch jellyroll pan. Sprinkle with walnuts. Bake at 375°F. for 12-15 minutes. Loosen edges of cake and invert onto towel sprinkled with powered sugar. Roll cake and towel together. Cool. For Filling: Beat cream cheese, butter, and vanilla well. Beat in powered sugar. Unroll cake and spread with filling. Roll up cake with filling. Chill before serving.

Aline's Raspberry Fudge Cake

1 cup all-purpose flour ~ ¾ teaspoon baking powder
¼ teaspoon salt ~ 4 (1 ounce) semisweet chocolate squares
4 (1 ounce unsweetened chocolate squares ~ Cocoa
¾ cup plus 1 Tablespoon butter or margarine ~ ¾ cup sugar
1 cup seedless raspberry jam ~ ¼ cup cherry juice
3 large eggs ~ Fresh raspberries for garnish

Grease a 9-inch springform pan and dust with cocoa then set aside. Combine flour, baking powder, and salt and set aside. Melt 3 semisweet chocolate squares, 4 unsweetened chocolate squares, and ¾ cup butter in a heavy saucepan over low heat, stirring constantly. Whisk together sugar, ¾ cup jam, cherry juice, and eggs in a large bowl. Stir in melted chocolate mixture and flour mixture then pour into prepared springform pan. Bake at 350°F. For 40 to 45 minutes or until set. Cool in pan on a wire rack for 10 minutes before removing sides of pan. For icing: melt remaining 1 semisweet chocolate square and 1 Tablespoon butter in a saucepan over low heat, stirring constantly. Let stand 15 to 20 minutes or until a good consistency for drizzling. Meanwhile spread the remaining ¼ cup jam over the top of cake. Slice the cake and place on individual dessert plates. Drizzle chocolate glaze over slices.

Grandmother Ada's
Sweet Potato Pudding

1 large raw sweet potato ~ 1 cup sugar ~ 1½ cup milk
½ cup butter, melted ~ 3 eggs, well beaten
2 teaspoons lemon flavoring ~ ¼ teaspoon salt

Finely grate sweet potato. Place in microwaveable dish and cover tightly. Cook on HIGH for 5 minutes, stirring once. Add remaining ingredients and cook on HIGH for 5 to 8 minutes, stirring once. Place in buttered baking dish and cook for 20 to 25 minutes on 50% power.

Easter Dinner

Easter Dinner in the South most often consists of a large ham and fresh vegetable dishes. The day isn't celebrated like it once was, with reverence and reflection. More often it is a time to head to the beach to enjoy a relatively cool late Spring holiday. In the backwoods there are still those that get dressed in their finery for church services followed by an Easter Dinner feast. This recipe remembers those that remember the real reason that we celebrate Easter in the South.

Easter Baked Ham

When choosing your Easter Ham remember that there are many types of hams to choose from. If you choose a bone-in ham (still on the bone) you can estimate 2-3 servings per pound of ham. If you choose a bone-out, precooked, or canned ham you can estimate 3-4 servings per pound of ham. Plan on cooking your ham a minimum of 15 minutes per pound, whether it is a precooked ham or not.

Place ham in a baking bag or cover with foil. Pour ½ inch of water in a baking pan. Place ham on rack. Bake in 325°F. oven 15 minutes per pound. During the last hour of baking remove ham from oven and cover with pineapple slices and secure with toothpicks. Sprinkle with brown sugar and ground cloves.

Douse the ham slices with a warm Raisin Sauce. Some family members might not like the keyword ingredient in this sauce. Save the raisins for last, serving those who prefer their sauce *without*, first.

Raisin Sauce

½ cup packed brown sugar ~ 1 Tablespoon cornstarch
1½ teaspoons dry mustard ~ ½ teaspoon ground cloves
¼ cup raisins ~ 1 Tablespoon margarine or butter
1 cup water ~ 2 Tablespoons lemon juice

Mix water, lemon juice, and margarine in saucepan over medium heat. Add all dry ingredients stirring until mix comes to a boil. Add raisins and simmer 2 to 3 minutes, stirring occasionally. Pour over ham slices.

Prepare traditional Southern vegetables like Plantation Sweet Potato Pone or Yam Soufflé to serve with the ham. Also make some good old-fashioned Southern rolls or cornbread. Light pies are preferred, to compliment the heavy meal. Serve homemade Peach Delight or Old Southern Berry Shrub with the meal.

Plantation Sweet Potato Pone

2 cups sweet potatoes, raw, finely grated
1 cup evaporated milk ~ 2 eggs, well beaten
¾ cup dark corn syrup ~ ¼ cup melted butter
1 teaspoon grated lemon rind ~ 2 teaspoons lemon juice
½ teaspoon salt ~ ½ teaspoon nutmeg
½ teaspoon cinnamon ~ ½ cup brown sugar

Grate potatoes into a large bowl with the milk to prevent them from darkening. Mix ingredients in order given. Pour into a greased shallow baking pan. Bake in a 350°F. oven for 30 minutes. Remove from oven and stir with a fork, then return to oven and bake 15 minutes longer until brown and crusty on top.

Poppie's Yam Soufflé

4 cups sweet potatoes, mashed ~ ¼ cup butter, softened
½ cup sugar ~ 3 eggs, beaten ~ ¼ teaspoon salt
¼ cup walnuts, chopped (or any other available nuts)

In a large mixing bowl, beat together yams, butter, sugar, eggs, and salt until fluffy. Turn into baking dish and sprinkle with nuts. Bake at 350°F. For 45 minutes. Serve hot.

Old Southern Berry Shrub

1 pound fresh blackberries or raspberries
2 cups apple cider vinegar ~ 2 cups sugar

Place berries in a non-metal bowl. Add vinegar to berries. Cover tightly with plastic wrap and set aside to macerate for 3 days. Strain mixture through a fine strainer into a medium saucepan, pressing down on berries to extract all the liquid. Discard pulp. Stir in sugar, boiling for 2-3 minutes, then remove from heat and cool. Store in a jar with a tight-fitting lid. To prepare each serving, combine ¼ cup berry concentrate with 1 cup ice water, pouring over ice in tall glasses. This recipe makes about 3 cups of concentrate or enough for about 12 servings.

Myrrh's Peach Delight

2 cups frozen peach slices, thawed
1 cup lemon flavored sparkling mineral water
½ teaspoon ginger, ground ~ 16 ounces lemon yogurt
ground nutmeg or cinnamon for garnish

Combine peaches, mineral water, and ground ginger in container of an electric blender. Cover and process until smooth. Pour mixture into a small pitcher and gently stir in yogurt. Garnish with nutmeg or cinnamon. This recipe doubles to yield 8 cups.

Happy New Years Hoppin' John

In the old days we might not have had much for New Years but leftovers from Christmas, yet we always had a big pot of Hoppin' John. In each pot the cook would deposit a penny. The person who got the bowl with the penny was assured of extra good luck for the entire year. Whatever else you serve for New Years, make sure you don't forget this recipe!

1 pound dried black-eyed peas ~ 2 medium onions
2 cups boiled ham, sliced thick and cubed
3 cloves garlic, large ~ 2 bay leaves ~ 3 ribs celery, diced
1 cup converted long-grain white rice ~ 3 scallions, sliced
1 10-ounce can diced tomatoes with chiles
1 large red bell pepper, diced ~ ¾ teaspoon salt
2 teaspoons Creole seasoning (optional)
¾ teaspoon dried thyme leaves ~ 1 clean penny

In a large pot, combine the black-eyed peas, ham, and 6 cups water. Cut 1 onion in half and add it to the pot along with the garlic and bay leaves. Bring to a boil then reduce the heat and simmer gently until the beans are tender but not mushy, 2-2½ hours. Drain the peas and ham and set aside. Remove and discard the bay leaves, onion, and garlic. Next, add 2½ cups of water to the pot and bring to a boil. Add the rice, cover, and simmer until the rice is almost tender, about 12 minutes. Mince the remaining onion. Add to the rice along with the peas and ham, tomatoes and their juices, bell pepper, celery, optional Creole seasoning, thyme, and salt. Cook until the rice is tender, 5 to 7 minutes. Stir in the sliced scallions. Just before serving drop a clean penny into the pot and stir.

MARDI GRAS

History

Mardi Gras may be the only holiday that Southerner's can claim as all their own. It is not celebrated in every city across the South but most Southern port cities have some sort of Mardi Gras celebration. To understand Mardi Gras one must briefly revisit the history of New Orleans. Small villages of the Quinipissa and Tangipahoa peoples were located in the vicinity of present-day New Orleans when the site was first visited in 1682 by a European explorer, Frenchman Réne-Robert Cavelier. In 1699, another French explorer, Jean Baptiste Le Moyne, returned to the site. Recognizing the importance of the location Baptiste Le Moyne established the first European settlement in New Orleans in 1718, after becoming governor of the Louisiana Territory. He named it Nouvelle Orléans, for the duc d'Orléans, regent of France. The story goes that the first Mardi Gras came to New Orleans by way of Baptiste in 1699. It is unlikely that the celebration really took shape until the mid-1700s. Early explorers are said to have celebrated this French Holiday along the banks of the Mississippi River.

Mardi Gras is the pre-Lenten festival celebrated in Roman Catholic countries and communities. In a strict sense, Mardi Gras is celebrated by the French as the last three days of Shrovetide and is a time of preparation immediately before Ash Wednesday and the start of the fast of Lent. It is thus the last opportunity for merrymaking and indulgence in food and drink. In practice, Mardi Gras is celebrated for at least a full week before Lent. It is marked by spectacular parades featuring floats, pageants, elaborate costumes, masked balls, and dancing in the streets.

Over the years, Orleanians have added to the celebration by establishing *krewes* (organizations) which host parades and balls. Carnival quickly became an exciting holiday for both children and adults. During the last century the celebration spread across the Southern Gulf Coast with annual observances held from Pensacola to Galveston.

Mardi Gras, French for "Fat Tuesday," is celebrated on Tuesdays for that reason. Of course the parties start long before Fat Tuesday. The Carnival season officially begins on January 6th or the *"Twelfth Night,"* also known to Christians as the *"Epiphany."* The actual date of Mardi Gras can fall between February 3 and March 9 depending on the Catholic Church's calendar. Mardi Gras is always 47 days before Easter Sunday.

The official colors for Mardi Gras are purple, green, and gold. The colors where chosen in 1872 by the King of Carnival, Rex. He chose the colors to stand for: Justice (purple), Faith (green), and Power (gold).

The Mardi Gras "season" begins about two weeks before Fat Tuesday. During those two weeks, parades can be viewed nightly. Almost all businesses are closed for Lundi Gras (Fat Monday) and for Mardi Gras itself. People travel from all over the world to New Orleans to enjoy this most extravagant of holidays.

Parades

Parades are put on by carnival krewes. Every year, each krewe picks a king and a queen who reign for their parade. The floats which are pulled by tractors are decorated to depict different themes. Most parades attract thousands of people hoping to catch beads, doubloons, cups or trinkets thrown from the floats by members of the krewe. Following the parade, the krewe usually has a ball featuring their king and queen, and their royal court. The royal court includes maids, dukes, pages, captains, and jesters.

Beads, Doubloons, Cups, and Trinkets

Most go to the parades hoping to go home with some of the famous catches. Most can easily obtain Mardi Gras gifts by shouting the famous phrase, *"Throw me somethin', mista!"*.

Beads are plastic necklaces that come in all different colors, shapes and sizes. They resemble jewels that royalty would wear. Doubloons are metal coins that are about the size of a silver dollar. They come in different colors and are stamped with the krewe's emblem and their theme for the year. Similar to doubloons, cups also bear the krewe's emblem and theme for the year. They are generally plastic drinking cups emblazoned with gold writing. Trinkets are known as everything else thrown from a float. This can include candy, stuffed animals, Frisbees, spears, roses, balls, and whistles.

Anywhere in the South around the time of Mardi Gras one can find a variety of amazing Mardi Gras dishes. Perhaps the most famous is the Kings Cake.

History of the King Cake

Legend has it that the King Cake derives its significance from the Epiphany. Epiphany comes from a Greek word that means "to show." Bethlehem is where the Infant Jesus first showed Himself to the world. As a symbol of this Holy Day, a tiny plastic baby is placed inside of each King Cake. The King Cake tradition is thought to have been brought to New Orleans from France around 1870.

A King Cake is an oval-shaped bakery delicacy; a cross between a coffee cake and a French pastry that is as rich in flavor as it is in history. It's decorated in the royal colors described above; purple for justice, green for faith, and gold for power. The King Cake's colors and shape are meant to resemble a jeweled crown, honoring the Wise Men who visited the Christ Child on Epiphany.

In the past, such things as coins, beans, pecans, or peas were hidden inside each King Cake. Today a tiny plastic baby is the common prize. At a party, the King Cake is sliced and served. Each person looks to see if their piece contains the baby. If so, then that person is named "King" for a day, and bound by custom to host the next party and provide the next King Cake!

Carnival season brings the height of demand for King Cakes, but some people eat them all year round! No Mardi Gras season would be complete without at least one King Cake. Treat yourself or surprise someone with one of these two fresh and delicious King Cakes recipes. The first is the "easy" version. The second will dirty just about every dish in your kitchen, not to mention trying your patience and Southern genteelness!

King Cake I
Quick & Easy

1 can cinnamon rolls, with icing
¾ cup of sugar, separated into
3 parts of ¼ each
food coloring
small (1-inch) plastic baby doll

Separate the cinnamon rolls and roll them out by hand so that they look like hot dogs. Shape the roll into an oval, then pinch the ends together and place on a cookie sheet. Bake as directed. While the cinnamon rolls are baking, use food coloring to dye sugar. Make one part purple using blue and red, one part green, and one part gold using yellow. When cinnamon rolls are finished cooking, insert the plastic baby doll into the cake. Ice the top with the white icing. Sprinkle the different colors of sugars alternating as you go around the oval. Serve cool.

King Cake II
Traditional New Orleans Recipe

½ cup war water (110 to 115°F.) ~ 2 packages active dry yeast
½ cup plus 1 teaspoon sugar ~ 3½ - 4½ cups flour unsifted
1 teaspoon nutmeg ~ 2 teaspoons salt
1 teaspoon lemon zest ~ ½ cup warm milk ~ 5 egg yolks
1 stick butter, cut into slices and softened,
plus 2 Tablespoons more softened butter
1 egg slightly beaten with 1 Tablespoon milk
1 teaspoon cinnamon ~ 1 1-inch plastic baby doll

Pour the warm water into a small shallow bowl and sprinkle yeast and 2 teaspoons of sugar into it. Allow the yeast and sugar to rest for three minutes then mix thoroughly. Set bowl in a warm place, for ten minutes or until yeast bubbles up and mixture almost doubles up in volume. Combine 3½ cups of flour, the remaining sugar, nutmeg, and salt, and sift into a large mixing bowl. Stir in lemon zest. Separate center of mixture to form a hole and pour in yeast mixture and milk. Add egg yolks and using a wooden spoon slowly combine dry ingredients into the yeast/milk mixture. When mixture is smooth, beat in 8 Tablespoons of butter, 1 Tablespoon at a time and continue to beat 2 minutes or until dough can be formed into a medium soft ball.

Place ball of dough on a lightly floured surface and knead like bread. During this kneading, add up to 1 cup more of flour (1 Tablespoon at a time) sprinkled over the dough. When dough is no longer sticky, knead 10 minutes more until shiny and elastic.

Using a pastry brush, coat the inside of a large bowl evenly with one Tablespoon of softened butter. Place dough ball in the bowl and rotate until the entire surface is buttered. Cover bowl with a thick kitchen towel and place in a draft free spot for about 1½ hours, or until the dough doubles in volume. Using a pastry brush, coat a large baking sheet with one Tablespoon of butter and set aside.

Remove dough from bowl and place on a lightly floured surface. Using your fist, punch dough down with a heavy blow. Sprinkle cinnamon over the top, pat and shake dough into a cylinder (like a large kielbasa). Twist dough to form a curled cylinder and loop cylinder onto the buttered baking sheet. Pinch the ends together to complete the circle. Cover the dough with a towel and let it sit in a draft free spot for 45 minutes until the circle of dough doubles in volume. Preheat oven to 375°F.

Brush the top and sides of the cake with egg wash and bake on middle rack of oven for 25 to 35 minutes until golden brown. Place cake on wire rack to cool. Once cool, hide the plastic baby in the cake.

Colored Sugars

Green, purple, and yellow paste
12 Tablespoons sugar

Squeeze a dot of green past in the palm of your hand. Sprinkle 2 Tablespoons of sugar over the past and rub together quickly. Place this mixture on wax paper and wash hands to remove color. Repeat process for other 2 colors. Set colors aside.

Icing

3 cups confectioners sugar
¼ cup lemon juice
3-6 Tablespoons water

Combine sugar, lemon juice, and 3 Tablespoons water until smooth. If icing is too stiff, add more water until spreadable. Spread icing over the top of the cake. Immediately sprinkle the colored sugars in individual rows consisting of about 2 rows of green, purple, and yellow. Serve in 2½-inch slices.

If you thought the traditional King Cake was tough you won't even want to think about trying the Chocolate Doberge Cake. The Doberge is a rich and sinful chocolate lovers' dream cake. It is a great Louisiana original for serving during the indulgent Mardi Gras season. *Doberge*, is a corruption of the French "d'auberge," which in this context means "from the hearth." One thing is for sure, if you attempt this recipe, the kitchen, the hearth, and the whole dining area will be strewn with dirty dishes when you're through. Being a chocolate lover I think it is well worth the effort!

Chocolate Doberge Cake

2 cups cake flour, sifted ~ 1 teaspoon baking soda
1 teaspoon salt ~ 10 Tablespoons margarine
1½ cups sugar ~ 3 eggs, separated, whites beaten until stiff
1 cup buttermilk ~ 1¼ teaspoons vanilla
1½ (1 ounce) squares unsweetened chocolate, melted
1 teaspoon almond extract

Filling

2½ cups evaporated milk ~ 1¼ cups sugar
2 (1 ounce) squares semi-sweet chocolate
5 Tablespoons flour ~ 4 egg yolks
2 Tablespoons butter or margarine
1¼ teaspoon vanilla ~ ¼ teaspoon almond extract

Frosting

1¼ cups sugar ~ 1 cup evaporated milk
1½ (1 ounce) squares unsweetened chocolate
4 Tablespoons margarine ~ 1 teaspoon vanilla

Preheat oven to 300°F. Grease and flour 2 9-inch round cake pans. In a medium bowl, sift the flour, soda, and salt 3 times. Cream the margarine and sugar in a large mixing bowl, and add egg yolks, one

Chocolate Doberge Cake ~ continued

at a time. Gradually alternate adding the flour mixture and buttermilk, then add chocolate and mix well by beating about 3 minutes. Fold in the 3 beaten egg whites, vanilla, and almond extracts. Bake for 45 minutes or until done. After the cake cools, split each layer in have to make 4 thin layers.

To make filling, put milk and chocolate in a sauce pan and heat until chocolate is melted. In a bowl, combine sugar and flour. Make a paste by adding hot milk chocolate by Tablespoons to the sugar and flour, then return to saucepan. Stir over medium heat until thick. Add 4 egg yolks all at once and stir rapidly to completely blend. Cook 2 or 3 minutes more. Remove from heat and add butter, vanilla, and almond extract. Cool and spread on cake, layering as you go. Do not spread on top layer.

For frosting, combine sugar and milk in a heavy saucepan, and bring to a boil, stirring constantly. Reduce heat and simmer for 6 minutes without stirring. Remove from heat and blend in chocolate. Add margarine and vanilla and return to medium-low heat, cooking 1 or 2 minutes. Place in refrigerator to cool. Beat well, then spread on the top and sides of the cake.

Whew! That makes me tired just thinking about it. It is surely worth the effort at least once a year. There are hundreds of other Mardi Gras favorites that I could include but I've narrowed the list to a few of Louisiana's most unique and indulgent specialities; Crab or Shrimp Mold, Jambalaya, and Red Beans & Rice. These are recipes you'll find no where but in the Deep South.

Bridgette's Crab or Shrimp Mold

1 10¾-ounce can cream of mushroom soup
8 ounces cream cheese, softened
1 ¼-ounce envelope unflavored gelatin,
softened in ¼ cup water
1 bunch green onions, chopped
3 pounds cooked shrimp, coarsely chopped
or
1 pound crab meat
1 cup mayonnaise
1 Tablespoon lemon juice
Tabasco, to taste

Heat soup, undiluted, and mix in the cream cheese. Stir in softened gelatin and blend well. Fold in remaining ingredients and pour into a lightly-oiled mold. Chill until firm and serve with your favorite crackers.

Red Beans and Rice
Original Louisiana Recipe

1 pound red beans, washed, drained,
and soaked in water overnight, drained ~ 3 cups water
2 cloves garlic, chopped ~ ½ cup chopped celery
1 large bay leaf, crushed ~ 1 medium onion, chopped
½ cup cooking oil ~ Salt and pepper
1 pound smoked sausage, sliced
2 Tablespoons parsley, chopped ~ Steaming rice

Place beans in cold water in a 4-quart pot. Add garlic, celery, bay leaf, onion, and oil and bring to a boil. Reduce heat and simmer for about 2 hours. Add water as needed, stirring occasionally. Add salt, pepper, sausage, and parsley and continue cooking over low heat for about 1 hour. Serve over a mound of steaming rice.

Aunt Barbara's Jambalaya

¼ cup oil ~ 1 3-3½ pound fryer, cut up
1 pound pork sausage, cut into ¼-inch slices
1 teaspoon Creole seasoning ~ 2 teaspoons salt
2 large onions, chopped ~ 2 large ribs of celery, chopped
½ cup chopped bell pepper ~ 3 cloves garlic, chopped
1 8-ounce can tomato sauce ~ 1 teaspoon salt
2 tablespoons chopped parsley ~ 4 cups cooked rice
2 tablespoons chopped green onion tops
1 6-ounce can water chestnuts, drained and chopped (optional)

Heat oil in a large, thick pot on medium-high heat. Add chicken pieces, brown on all sides and cook until tender (20-25 minutes). Add sausage, Creole seasoning, and salt. Cover, lower heat, and cook until chicken is well-done, about 30 minutes.

Remove chicken and sausage and drain all except ⅓ of the drippings from the pot. Add onions, celery, bell pepper, and garlic. Sauté until tender. Stir in tomato sauce and salt and return chicken (deboned if preferred) and sausage to the pot. Cover and simmer about 10 minutes. Add the parsley and green onion tops, cooking an additional 5 minutes, covered. Fold in cooked rice (and optional water chestnuts) and simmer about 10 minutes. Serve piping hot.

Index

A

Asparagus
Asparagus Casserole, 40
Asparagus with Cashew
Butter, 111
Aunt Barbara's Jambalaya, 192

B

Bell Peppers
Stuffed Bell Peppers, 50
Stuffed Bell Peppers II, 103
Beverages
Coffee Punch, 74
Cranberry Tea, 20
Gingerberry Punch, 21
Myrrh's Peach Delight, 181
Old Southern Berry
Shrub, 181
Rich Coffee Punch, 74
Sassafras Tea, 73
Southern Cider, 74
Spiced Citrus Tea, 19
Strawberry Soup, 18
Summer Iced Tea, 18
Tangy Spiced Tea, 19
Tea Syrup, 20
Biscuits
Baby Biscuits, 33
Chocolate Biscuits
of Doom, 128
Corned Beef & Tomato

Biscuits, 97
Meal-Sized Biscuits , 30
Mississippi River
Biscuits, 32
Plain Biscuits, 31
Quick Mix Biscuits, 31
Sausage-Sage Stuffed
Biscuits, 101
Black Bean & Rice Salad, 40
Blueberries
Blueberry Crunch, 128
Blueberry Pineapple
Surprise, 128
Blueberry Salad, 117
Blueberry Sour Cream
Muffins, 136
Rich Blueberry
Muffins , 100
Breads
Banana Nut Bread, 135
Cracklin' Bread, 97
Grandma's Homemade
Rolls, 98
Herbed Onion Bread, 98
Spoon Rolls, 99
Sweet Potato Bread, 100
Breakfasts
Apple Raisin Bars, 36
Baby Biscuits, 33
Cheese Grits, 27
Chocolate Pancakes, 35

G

H

J

R

S

Everything begins and ends with cotton. . . or at least it used to!

Need a Gift?

For

- **Shower** • **Birthday** • **Mother's Day** •
- **Anniversary** • **Christmas** •

Turn Page For Order Form
(Order Now While Supply Lasts!)

To Order Copies Of

SOUTHERN HOMEMADE

Please send me _____copies at $11.95 each.   _____
Add $3.50 for shipping and handling per book.   _____
                                    Total: _____

(Make checks payable to **QUIXOTE PRESS.**)

Name_____

Street_____

City _____ State _____ Zip_____

Send Orders To:
Hearts 'N' Tummies Cookbook Co.
3544 Blakslee St.
Wever, IA 52658
1-800-571-2665

- -

To Order Copies Of

SOUTHERN HOMEMADE

Please send me _____copies at $11.95 each.   _____
Add **$3.50** for shipping and handling per book.   _____
                                    Total: _____

(Make checks payable to **QUIXOTE PRESS.**)

Name_____

Street_____

City _____ State _____ Zip_____

Send Orders To:
Hearts 'N' Tummies Cookbook Co.
3544 Blakslee St.
Wever, IA 52658
1-800-571-2665